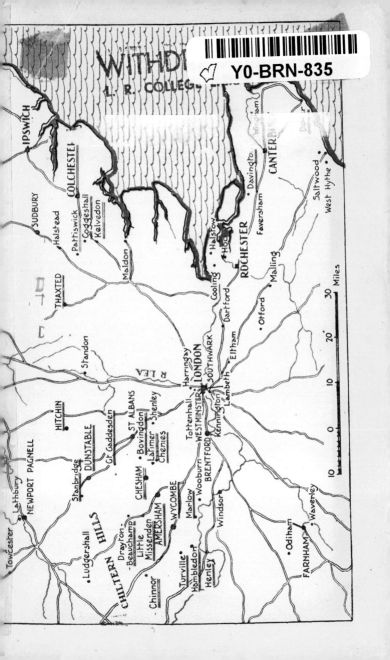

JOHN WYCLIFFE

and the

Beginnings of English Nonconformity

is one of the volumes
in the

TEACH YOURSELF HISTORY
LIBRARY

Edited by A. L. ROWSE

Teach Yourself History

JOHN WYCLIFFE

and the

Beginnings of
English Nonconformity

by

K. B. McFARLANE

NEW YORK
THE MACMILLAN COMPANY
1953

To

HELENA

for whom the book was written

901
R79W

31734
Oct. 1954

PRINTED IN GREAT BRITAIN

A General Introduction to the Series

THIS series has been undertaken in the conviction that there can be no subject of study more important than history. Great as have been the conquests of natural science in our time—such that many think of ours as a scientific age *par excellence*—it is even more urgent and necessary that advances should be made in the social sciences, if we are to gain control of the forces of nature loosed upon us. The bed out of which all the social sciences spring is history; there they find, in greater or lesser degree, subject-matter and material, verification or contradiction.

There is no end to what we can learn from history, if only we would, for it is coterminous with life. Its special field is the life of man in society, and at every point we can learn vicariously from the experience of others before us in history.

To take one point only—the understanding of politics: how can we hope to understand the world of affairs around us if we do not know how it came to be what it is? How to understand Germany, or Soviet Russia, or the United States—or ourselves, without knowing something of their history?

There is no subject that is more useful, or indeed indispensable.

Some evidence of the growing awareness of this may be seen in the immense increase in the interest of the reading public in history, and the much larger place the subject has come to take in education in our time.

This series has been planned to meet the needs and demands of a very wide public and of education—they are indeed the same. I am convinced that the most congenial, as well as the most concrete and practical, approach to history is the biographical, through the lives of the great men whose actions have been so much part of history, and whose careers in turn have been so moulded and formed by events.

The key idea of this series, and what distinguishes it from any other that has appeared, is the intention by way of a biography of a great man to open up a significant historical theme; for example, Cromwell and the Puritan Revolution, or Lenin and the Russian Revolution.

My hope is, in the end, as the series fills out and completes itself, by a sufficient number of biographies to cover whole periods and subjects in that way. To give you the history of the United States, for example, or the British Empire or France, *via* a number of biographies of their leading historical figures.

That should be something new, as well as convenient and practical, in education.

I need hardly say that I am a strong believer in people with good academic standards writing once more for the general reading public, and of the public being given the best that the universities can provide. From this point of view this series is intended to bring the university into the homes of the people.

A. L. ROWSE.

ALL SOULS COLLEGE,
OXFORD.

Contents

Author's Note

THANKS are due and are gratefully offered: to Mr. A. B. Emden, lately Principal of St. Edmund Hall, for answering many questions about graduate Lollards; to Mr. W. A. Pantin for putting at my disposal his photostats of two unpublished works by Ughtred Boldon; to Dr. C. H. Thompson for allowing me to borrow the typescript of his Manchester Ph.D. thesis on Boldon from Professor E. F. Jacob; to Miss Kathleen Major, Mrs. J. Varley, Miss Dorothy M. Williamson and Mr. D. McN. Lockie for easing my access to the sources; to my colleague Mr. Karl Leyser for his generous help and criticism; and to Dr. J. R. L. Highfield of Merton College for reading and commenting upon the book in manuscript.

A brief note on sources and some suggestions for further reading will be found at the end.

K. B. McFarlane.

Magdalen College,
    Oxford.

Prologue

IF you should wish to teach yourself medieval history
you must learn first that the sources, though often
abundant, are patchy, voluminous on some topics, entirely
absent for others. It is possible, for example, to investigate
the day-to-day workings of Richard II's treasury and courts
of law, and yet still to be unable to solve the problem
that has long baffled the student: What sort of character
had Richard, what were his springs of action? The
materials for administrative history survive in overwhelm-
ing plenty; but those details on which can be based an
understanding of aims, a judgement of motives and an
imaginative grasp of personality are utterly lacking. As
a great medievalist recently complained: 'We know so
little about these people. As we stir these cold ashes, a
tongue of flame seems to dart out and flicker and die.
We cannot feel sure of very much.'

For this reason it is unlikely that it will ever be possible to write a life, a real life, of Wycliffe. Too many of
the essential ingredients have been lost. For one thing
we are seriously handicapped by not knowing such pieces
of purely factual information as when he was born, who
his parents were and how he was reared. Indeed, we
know very little about the external events of Wycliffe's
career at any stage; we merely catch a series of glimpses,
sometimes with the added uncertainty that the John
Wycliffe we are pursuing may turn out to be another man
of the same name. Our subject's appearances are at the
best intermittent and the gaps are long.

Still, this would not matter so much had we a firm
grasp of the character of the man and knew what he was
out to do. Unfortunately, he has left us very little guid-
ance. Like many other medieval scholars, he was a
copious writer. His printed works—and a fair number
are still in manuscript—occupy about forty substantial

volumes. Yet they are for the most part so impersonal that one gathers little more from them than that their author was learned, subtle, ingenious, opinionated, tirelessly argumentative and rather humourless. That is perhaps something. But they throw scarcely any light on his reasons for acting as he did and they contain practically no material at all of an autobiographical nature. The result is that the many interpretations of his character and career that have been published—and he has been the subject of more biographies than probably any other medieval Englishman—are based largely on guesswork.

There might be slight harm in that if the guesses were appropriate, but most of them are not. This arises partly from their authors' want of knowledge of the England in which Wycliffe lived, partly from a hagiographical intention. The lives they have written have been works of edification rather than of history, in which the nonconformist saint, a good deal larger than life-size, is pictured against a fantastically improbable background. The first task of an impartial biographer must therefore be destructive: to free his subject from a great deal of ignorant repainting and several layers of rich brown protestant varnish. What remains after this has been done may be disappointing, but it is all that is left of the original. There will doubtless be those who hold that the picture has been ruined in the process.

In the absence of detailed information about Wycliffe's life the best way to estimate the importance of his achievement is by measuring his impact on his times. From the nature of that impact it is possible to deduce something about the force responsible for it. A sceptical French historian, pardonably annoyed by the incense of the Wycliffolaters, has doubted whether the impression made was very great. But those in the best position to know, Wycliffe's own contemporaries, would not have agreed with Professor Perroy. Heretics were rare in medieval England; and the founder of a heretical sect which believed itself capable of tumbling Henry V from his throne and defied all attempts to stamp it out cannot be regarded as negligible. English nonconformity owes its origins, humble though these may have been, to Master John Wycliffe. For that reason, if for no other, his fortunes and those of his disciples would be worthy of study. But there is another reason: the response of those in authority to Wycliffe's challenge is as instructive as it was unanimous. Thanks to Wycliffe we have a better understanding of those twin-engines of late medieval government: the English Church and the English State.

Chapter One

Wycliffe and Oxford

WHEN he died on 31 December 1384 John Wycliffe was about fifty-five years of age. By contemporary standards therefore he was a moderately old man. Yet until its last decade his life, though it had brought him distinction of a modest sort among his fellow-scholars, had been quite unremarkable and save for what was to follow would have attracted little posthumous notice. Had his death occurred in 1374 or even as much as a year or two later Wycliffe would be remembered only by specialist historians as one of the lesser ornaments of medieval Oxford. They would know him as the author of a number of philosophical works of no particular brilliance though of sustained competence, several of which, despite his enormous reputation, have not yet been found worthy of print. To the common reader he would be no more familiar than are those two precursors to whom he was most indebted, Bradwardine and FitzRalph, which is as much as to say not at all. It was only when this middle-aged doctor of divinity abandoned his crowded lecture-room for the royal service that there began that period of frenzied agitation upon which his later fame depends.

Even then it was not at once apparent that anything abnormal was to be expected. For a successful theologian to seek more profitable employment for his talents in the king's pay was usual enough. It was only when he decided, some eight years at most before his death, to propagate his unorthodox views among the ill-educated laity that Wycliffe's progress became definitely eccentric. From the very nature of their speculations medieval scholars were apt to fall into heresy, but the range of their influence did not ordinarily extend beyond the walls of the universities in which they taught; their profundities were too deep to be plumbed by any but their academic equals and the last thing they desired was a popular following. It was the extra-mural character of Wycliffe's appeal that gave it its marked singularity. He came to be the revered leader of men who could neither grasp his reasoning nor even, indeed, understand that Latin language in which it was normally expressed. It was for this betrayal of his order that he was most bitterly denounced by his academic opponents. His first disciples were learned popularisers; they invited the common man to spurn his official pastors and to teach himself heresy; and to help him in the work they translated the Bible and composed simple vernacular statements of their faith. They were different from the other clerical agitators with which the fourteenth century abounded, in that they were university-trained members of an intellectual *élite*; moreover, their leader was generally recognised to be the most outstanding scholar of his day. That such men should inspire and foster a heretical movement among the lesser clergy and the laity was rather as if a group of barons had stirred up a peasants' revolt.

For in Wycliffe's England the church was ruled by an aristocracy of graduates. In this respect it did not reflect faithfully the social order of which it was a part. Its members were recruited from the free, and promotion depended upon a combination of birth, influence and talent in much the same way as it did in the lay world. But unless a clerk possessed an aptitude for those forms of study which the universities offered he was unlikely to go far. It was, of course, possible for an exceptionally able man to rise to the top without a degree; the royal service, though to a much less extent than formerly, could still prove a useful ladder to a talented administrator. But the number of bishops who had started life as clerks in a government office was small and still decreasing. Those royal servants who were rewarded with a mitre were usually graduates who had entered the administration at what we should now call ministerial level, over the heads of the permanent staff. Success, it is clear, depended most of all upon educational opportunity. A yeoman's son, perhaps even a bondman's son, might rise to the primacy if he were fortunate enough to get someone, either an individual or a corporation, to finance his residence at the university. It is difficult to measure what the chances were; certainly a good few of Wycliffe's contemporaries who reached the episcopal bench had achieved their promotion from humble homes. More and more of the richer benefices, the canonries, prebends and cathedral dignities, went to a select number of well-educated, sometimes learned, graduates who added diplomatic or administrative experience to an exacting intellectual discipline, whose time was taken up exclusively with the government of church and state and whose pastoral or choral duties were delegated to an inferior class. Upon this clerical proletariat fell most of the ill-paid dirty work of the church. As curates to absentee rectors, as vicars-choral to pluralist canons, as chantry priests and mass-singers for a fee, as the incumbents of the very poorest livings, the vast majority of clerks laboured for small reward and without hope of advancement. Though no unfreed villein might be admitted to holy orders, churchmen, like their lay counterparts, were divided into the two nations of masters and men. The masters were the masters of arts.

In this world John Wycliffe was no under-dog. By the time he reached his early forties, he was on the threshold of the highest honours. His career at Oxford, in every way a notable one, had marked him out for the king's service and the rich preferment with which that service was commonly rewarded. He is first met with in 1356 as a junior fellow of Merton College. This and the dates at which he took his higher degrees make it likely that he was born about 1330 or perhaps a little after. Nothing definite is known about his parentage and early upbringing. A late and possibly untrustworthy local tradition connects him with the village of Wycliffe, near Richmond, in the north riding of Yorkshire, and states that he was born at Hipswell, a few miles to its south-east. This has been made the foundation for a vast edifice of conjecture which would identify him with the head of the family which held the manor and advowson of Wycliffe for many centuries. While there is nothing inherently impossible in this identification, it is more likely than not to be mistaken. The most we are justified in believing is that he came from the neighbourhood of Richmond and that he was probably a member of the modest land-owning family that bore his name. But for the fact that his later patron, John of Gaunt, was the feudal overlord of that area between 1342 and 1372 and therefore the natural protector of its aspiring sons, it would not much signify what his origins were. In his youth at least he could pass as a poor scholar in need of financial assistance, and in common with not a few of his contemporaries, both lay and clerical, he had the ability to make his own way. If any of the vernacular writings ascribed to him were actually from his pen—which is disputable—they betray nothing of his social or geographical background. Whoever wrote them almost certainly spoke the standard educated English of his time.

The fact that the reformer was first of all a schoolman with a particular kind of training is of fundamental importance to an understanding of his career. Wycliffe the political agitator and Wycliffe the founder of a heretical sect never lost touch with Wycliffe the don. That he was at least fifty before he was finally driven from the university makes it important that we should have some picture of what Wycliffe's Oxford was.

Needless to say, the medieval university was almost unrecognisably different from what has grown out of it in the course of the last six hundred years. Take, for example, the colleges: in 1360 there were six which, according to the most reliable estimate, contained altogether fewer than seventy-five members. Of these only ten were undergraduates, all at Exeter, and even there not admitted until the third year of their B.A. course. The rest had already taken at least a bachelor's degree and the majority were masters. There were no undergraduate scholars in the modern sense of the word and commoners were unknown. It is no exaggeration to say that colleges were, in the words of Dr. H. E. Salter, 'really external to the university—

backwaters not in the main stream, as now are Campion Hall and Ruskin College'.

Apart from these six colleges for the secular clergy, there existed in Wycliffe's time a number of houses to which monks and friars were sent to receive the advantages of a university training. Because they were swept away or turned to new uses at the Reformation, their importance has often been seriously underestimated by Oxford's later historians. The monastic orders having developed their own intellectual traditions before universities existed were at first inclined to hold aloof from a new learning which emphasised philosophy, theology and law at the expense of literature and history. They were, too, reluctant that their members should be exposed, as they were almost bound to be at Oxford, to the temptations of a less secluded discipline. But by the 1360s their conservatism had broken down and there were three Benedictine priories or halls, frequently called colleges, and a Cistercian abbey, in which the more promising monks from the English monasteries could reside to attend the schools. Mainly for financial reasons, the number in residence at any one time was not large; in 1360, all told, it probably did not much exceed fifty.

The mendicant friars, on the other hand, had played a conspicuous part in the life of the university ever since their arrival in England little over a century before Wycliffe's birth. Robert Grosseteste, Oxford's first chancellor, became the Franciscans' lecturer, and many of the scholars who made the university renowned throughout Europe, including Roger Bacon, Duns Scotus and William Ockham, were friars. If the secular colleges could retort a little later with FitzRalph, Bradwardine and Wycliffe they still had the worse of the contest. It is small wonder that they got their own back in post-Reformation times by claiming their successful rivals for themselves; that is why a highly imaginative portrait of Duns Scotus still hangs in Merton's hall. Nor were the friars only scholars and preachers, for such outstanding English churchmen as Archbishops Kilwardby and Patcham were products of their Oxford schools. This pre-eminence, won so spectacularly in the first century of their existence, survived into Wycliffe's day, and many of his early allies and later intellectual opponents were doctors drawn from the four great mendicant societies. In 1360 there were about 270 friars in Oxford, of whom probably something like eighty were students.

At most times in the fourteenth century there were between twelve and fifteen hundred clerks in residence at the university, but the bulk of them were neither fellows of colleges, monks nor friars. Readers of Chaucer will, I hope, remember that his poor scholar of Oxford, who was so good a weather-prophet, lodged in the house of John the carpenter. Farcical though the incidents of the *Miller's Tale* are—I doubt whether landlords were cuckolded more often then than now—it is full of accurate and probably first-hand local colour. Like 'hënde Nicholas' and most students today in other universities than Oxford and Cambridge, the great majority of graduates and undergraduates lived all their time in private houses in the town. The richer sort might bring or employ a private tutor and rent a house of their own. The commonest thing, however, was for a master of arts to take a lease of one of the larger tenements, which would then be registered, year by year so long as he occupied it, as an academic 'hall'. Here he would provide board, lodging and tuition for anything up to fifteen or twenty students at standard prices; and often act *in loco parentis,* doling out pocket-money and keeping a fatherly eye upon the morals of his younger charges.

There were a great many of these halls, which tended to specialise. Thus there were halls for those taking the arts course, halls for lawyers, for northerners and southerners, for Welsh and Irish, each with a goodwill which was worth selling to an incoming tenant. Though the institution has long vanished, some of the buildings still survive behind modern shop-fronts, the best preserved being Tackley's Inn just west of Oriel in High Street. Even in the middle ages the shops were usually already there, with cellars beneath them also let out to tradesmen; those adjoining Tackley's Inn in 1363 were occupied by a wine-vault, a candlestick-maker and a taper-seller. A more distracting neighbour might be a brothel. Such halls were approached by narrow passages, many of which remain, and were therefore themselves sometimes called 'entries'. Others—the larger ones—directly overlooked the streets.

The landlords were called principals. The accommodation they provided was invariably modest and in the main devoid of privacy. A typical hall would contain a largish refectory, a separate chamber for the principal and half a dozen smaller rooms on the upper floors, each holding four undergraduates or two or three bachelors. Only a senior was likely to have a bed, let alone a room, of his own; undergraduates 'chummed' together. If by modern standards these students' quarters were cramped, bare of furniture, cold and draughty in winter and stuffy and dark in summer, they did not compare unfavourably in these respects with contemporary domestic comfort everywhere. Chaucer's Nicholas, though conventionally described as poor, seems to have been unusually well-housed, since

> A chambre hadde he in that hostelrye
> Allone, withouten any compaignye,

with shelves of books at his bed-head, an astrolabe, a press for his clothes and a psaltery (or small harp); but then he had 'learned art' and therefore was presumably an M.A. Before he had achieved that status Wycliffe had been elected a probationer fellow of Merton, a small but well-endowed body of promising students who had at least taken their first degree. Its sole function, as it was that of all colleges then founded, was to provide needy scholars already at the university with the funds necessary to proceed to one of the higher degrees and a house in which they might lead a corporate life conducive to study. There was a means test, and as soon as a fellow received a benefice of more than a certain value he vacated his place to someone more deserving. Those elected were rarely so unlucky as to have to cling to their fellowships for long after their doctorates had been achieved.

Wycliffe's connection with Merton, which cannot have

been so very old in 1356, was a brief one, since at some time soon after that date and before the spring of 1360 he was elected third master of Balliol. Again he did not hold this position for long. His institution on 14 May 1361 to the college's fattest living, that of Fillingham in Lincolnshire, involved his resignation from the mastership. But it did not necessitate his departure from the university. Although he had recently taken his M.A. he was now working for the bachelorship in theology, and this entailed residence and study. He therefore hired a lodging in Queen's College, which was too poor to fill all its rooms with its own fellows and made a little revenue by letting those it did not need to well-to-do scholars like the rector of Fillingham. But for occasional absences and for the short time when he was warden of Canterbury, Wycliffe was a lodger in Queen's—though he was never in any strict sense a member of that college—until his final withdrawal from Oxford in 1381.

Meanwhile he was building himself a reputation in the public schools of the university. What that involved, though full of unsolved problems, must now be briefly described. Most popular descriptions of the medieval scholar are inclined for obvious reasons to give more prominence to the occupations of his leisure than to those of his working-hours. Nothing could be more out of place in a biography of Wycliffe, whose enormous industry can have left him little time for anything else. To introduce here an account of the sports and the low life of medieval Oxford would be like illustrating Mr. Gladstone's time at Christ Church entirely from the adventures of *Verdant Green*. And as a sap even Gladstone himself was hardly in the Wycliffe class.

On entering the university at fourteen or fifteen years of age the young clerk, who had already received the first tonsure that distinguished him from the unlettered laity, underwent no test of his fitness, either mental or moral, to read for a degree. Nor was he compelled to present himself for examination by a certain date; having qualified by sufficient residence and application, he proceeded to the next stage in his own time. The arts course, taken by all beginners, was what would now be called a general one, including grammar, arithmetic, geometry, astronomy and the theory (though not the practice) of music, but with the main emphasis on rhetoric, logic and the 'the three philosophies', natural, moral and metaphysical. Instruction was given in classes and by lectures in which set texts, mostly Latin translations from the works of Aristotle, were dictated, expounded and learnt by heart. Its most characteristic feature, however, was the disputation, in which a master or more senior pupil maintained a thesis against others in public argument. By the end of his third year, if all went well, the undergraduate was thought to be ready to join the bachelors in these exercises and became what was known as a 'questionist'. Nine months later those who were willing could undergo the examination upon which admission to the baccalaureate was decided.

This was conducted (as were all examinations) *viva voce*, and the candidate had to furnish evidence of his knowledge, morals and regularity in attendance which satisfied the four 'Masters of the Schools' appointed to test him. If he were successful and wished to persist with his studies, another three years had to elapse before he was allowed, after a similar but more thorough investigation, to supplicate for the degree of M.A. During this period, besides continuing to hear at least two lectures a week from his own teacher, he had himself to deliver a course on one of the books of Aristotle and to take part in the disputations both of his fellow-bachelors and of the masters. Finally, on taking his M.A. he had two more years of 'necessary regency' in which as a member of Congregation (the governing body of the university) he had many routine duties to perform and both lectured and disputed regularly.

After regency the more ambitious and intelligent were fit to leave arts for one of the higher faculties of medicine, law or theology. Since Wycliffe was a theologian the last may be taken as an example of this stage. The course for the B.D.—as the bachelorship in theology is generally called—took five years and that for the D.D. roughly another two. For the first the Bible had to be intensively studied and there were the usual disputations; for the second, disputations, preaching and lecturing. And as in the case of the M.A. the fully-fledged doctor was required to continue lecturing for a further two years after he had qualified for his degree. Candidates had to be 'of good report, honest conversation and sound body'. Whatever else they were, they were not raw. An undergraduate who had started at fifteen would be at least thirty-three before he had completed his training—unless, like some well-born lawyers, he succeeded in obtaining a dispensation to telescope parts of the course. Wycliffe was forty or over, having allowed his studies to be interrupted by administrative and other duties; although already a bachelor of arts in 1356, he did not take his D.D. apparently until 1372. Not a few others were similarly long.

A training as lengthy as this was bound to lead to many casualties. It has been reckoned that at Oxford in the fifteenth century only a third of the starters became bachelors and a sixth masters. Judging from the fact that parish priests often obtained leave of absence from their cures in order to frequent the university for as little as a year at a time, a number had no intention of going far. Sometimes marriage beckoned, sometimes comfortable employment. One difficulty was expense; idleness and vice were others; above all, lack of aptitude. The note against several names in the register of Winchester College to the effect that this or that *alumnus* had 'made up his mind to abandon study' tells a common tale of wilted resolution. Those who continued to the end were undoubtedly fit for leadership.

And as such they were treated by contemporary employers. For considered as an education for public life rather than as a scholar's apprenticeship this curriculum had much to be said for it. That it did not appeal to the humanists of the sixteenth century, whose abuse of the dunces and 'barking curs' of the old learning was as unscrupulous as it was effective, does not necessarily condemn it. Logic-choppers the medieval schoolmen certainly were and their Latin was most un-Ciceronian. But if in their long and exacting course they learnt a fine precision of thought and a language apt to express it, these were practical accomplishments for which worldly rulers, agreeing with Talleyrand that theologians make the best diplomatists, were prepared to pay highly. Although the subject-matter of their studies was totally irrelevant to their future tasks, the discipline which set so high a store by an accurate memory, the quick mastery of a complicated argument and a ready tongue in public debate was, after all, no bad training for a statesman.

As a method of acquiring wisdom scholasticism was perhaps less valuable; but even here a respectable case exists. The schoolmen themselves maintained that the practice of disputation was not only of service to education but also to knowledge. As one of them put it, 'this exercise is far more useful than reading, since by it doubts are resolved. Nothing is perfectly known which has not been masticated by the teeth of disputation'. Minds thus sharpened could not but be enquiring. The more one reads about medieval universities the less one can believe in that sedulous regard for authority which is often denounced as their gravest defect. On the contrary, it is only too clear that the anxious interference of papal and episcopal superiors, intermittent as it was bound to be, was quite ineffective as a check upon the speculative licence permitted in the schools. It was only when Wycliffe's heretical teaching threatened to subvert a whole university that the authorities brought themselves to decisive action against it. It is equally obvious that truth was served by definition, even if much of it was of the kind called hair-splitting. All the arguments about fixed fate, free will, foreknowledge absolute may have been as vain and false as later reformers declared, but only the prejudiced would maintain that the frontiers of the known were not thereby greatly advanced. A university of which it could be said that it produced a new logical system every twenty years was in no danger of stagnating beneath the dead weight of authority. If anything, a little less contentiousness would have been no loss. The direct observation of nature and the use of experimental techniques in science were neglected, it is true, though not nearly so neglected as is sometimes believed. History, too, was disregarded, being held a subject fitter for monks than for scholars, but this did not prevent Wycliffe and his contemporaries from drawing important lessons from a historical study of the church's doctrines; it was dislike of the changes introduced in the previous millennium which took them back to the Scriptures and thence to protestantism.

To reside for a number of years at Oxford a student evidently needed a good supply of money. Although prices were on the whole low, especially in the halls where they were regulated in the interests of the consumer, it must have been burdensome for a squire or a yeoman to have to maintain a son at the university even for the time necessary for the first degree in arts. A few notes of the terminal accounts rendered in 1424 at a hall kept by Mr. John Arundell, afterwards bishop of Chichester, have been accidentally preserved and show that it was possible for an undergraduate to get through the year on 50s. for board, lodging, tuition, clothes and even such extras as amusements. An M.A. would probably have needed about twice that amount; and anyone going on to the higher faculties might find the purchase of books a heavy additional strain. Model letters, composed by masters for the use of students, provide us with many details about the expenses of residence and about the academic life in general in our period. One example will serve; a student of Roman law is imagined to be writing thus to his father:

'Since I cannot get along here without great expense, I shall have hardly enough money to pay my way until the bearer of this letter returns. For not only can I not manage on less than 8d. a week for my board, but I have already spent my allowance on other necessities and have still not finished spending. Thus on my journey to Oxford for myself and my horse, 3s. 4d. Item on the purchase of two books at Oxford on my arrival . . . 6s. 8d. Item to the doctor from whom I hear my ordinary lectures, 2s. And when you reckon in the wages of our manciple and cook, the rent of my study and a great many other necessities which

I refrain from specifying because it would take too long, it should be obvious that my expenses are not unreasonable.

'Apart from this I think I ought to tell you one thing: that there have never been better conditions of work for those studying the civil law than there are this year; for there are two doctors continuously here lecturing where before there was only one. Each outbids the other to make the greater progress and to supply the more useful sort of teaching. In the hall where I am living the company is good and respectable and we have sound instruction; whence by God's grace and your help I shall make a happy ending to the work I have begun. Wherefore I am afraid I must ask you out of your benevolence to send me by the bearer of this letter whatever you can. Please also return me by the messenger a note of the amount you intend to allow me from time to time, and be sure this time to tell me the state of your health. . . .'

The burden of the majority of these letters was inevitably poverty. A young man was unlikely to go to the trouble and expense of procuring and copying anything so impressively formal as these Latin missives except when it was a case for a begging letter *de profundis*. Such finished and elegant products of the professional writer were expected to draw money from the stoniest heart. Then, as now, it was not always the poorest students who were those most deeply in debt. The evidence suggests that the majority were the sons of knightly, merchant and professional families whose parents could afford to keep them until they succeeded in obtaining a benefice; this, if accompanied by leave of absence for the purpose of further study, would enable them to be self-supporting, or nearly so, during their later years at the university. The genuinely poor could look hopefully for a wealthy patron to launch them on their studies and in due course to present them to the vacant livings in his gift. It was customary for bishops and temporal lords to finance a number of promising youths in this way, and even a monastic house might do the same. Thus we find Durham cathedral priory not only sending its monks to the college it maintained at Oxford, but paying for the education of secular clerks native to the diocese in which it and much of its land lay. It was indeed one of the obligations of lordship; and like most others it was capable of yielding a profitable return in loyal service. The local magnate who started a future prince of the church on his rise to wealth and power might have no reason to regret his discriminating charity. Finally, the ablest of the unbeneficed poor were provided for by the colleges, the scholars of which were drawn by their founders' injunctions from the counties in which their estates lay. Hence Wycliffe's connection with two colleges, Merton and Balliol, which were landowners in the north country. The 'tied' fellowships which were regarded as so scandalous in the nineteenth century therefore reflected the local patriotism and territorial connections dear to late medieval society. A college paid back the rents it drew from a particular county in the form of scholarships for local boys.

One other source of bounty remains to be mentioned. From time to time during the fourteenth century the university was in the habit of petitioning the pope to grant benefices to its more deserving graduates. Such requests were accompanied by a list of those thought distinguished enough to merit this form of recognition. In the petition of 24 November 1362 the name of John Wycliffe appeared as an aspirant to a canonry and prebend in York minster, the cathedral of his native diocese. His living of Fillingham was worth at least £20 a year, out of which he was expected to furnish a mass-priest to take his place during his absence from the parish; this, if he was conscientious, may have cost him a quarter of his stipend. The remainder, supposing that he had no other source of income, would have maintained him, though hardly in dignity or affluence, at the university. The rent of his chamber at Queen's was 20s. *per annum*; and even if his food and clothes could have been obtained for a few pounds, there cannot have been much over for a scholar's heaviest expenditure, that on ·books. It would not be generous therefore to describe the petition in his case as unjustified.

It was only partially successful. The pope's response was to grant him in 1362 a canonry and prebend (that of Aust) in the collegiate church of Westbury-on-Trym just outside Bristol. This did not entail residence, but the canon was required to provide a vicar to take his share of the services at Westbury and he was also responsible for maintaining the chancel at Aust in repair. The value of this benefice was rated (perhaps under-rated) at £6 13s. 4d. —that is to say, at very little more than the absentee canon would have had to pay his vicar. It is hardly surprising that, like the majority of his colleagues, Wycliffe failed to appoint one, while at the same time neglecting, as no doubt his predecessors had done, his duty to take care of the chancel at Aust. Unfortunately, in 1366 the bishop of Worcester, William Whittlesey, in whose diocese Westbury was, made an official visitation of the college. It was found that all five canons had been non-resident ever since they had been installed and that only one—not Wycliffe—had seen fit to employ a vicar. The defaulters were summoned to appear before the bishop and their revenues were meanwhile sequestrated. We do not know what followed, but the officious Whittlesey was soon after translated from Worcester to the primacy of Canterbury. What is certain is that Wycliffe retained his prebend of Aust in Westbury until his death; that when called upon by another bishop in 1366 to declare all the benefices he was enjoying he failed to make any response; and that there is no evidence that he either resided at Westbury or took his responsibilities there any more seriously thereafter than he had done at first.

That he was an absentee and a negligent pluralist, if only in a very small way compared with his more fortunate contemporaries, has naturally given rise to much unfavourable comment. Critics of abuses should doubtless be unusually careful not to commit the faults they castigate in others. The story of Wycliffe's behaviour over the prebend of Aust will warn us to expect a certain amount of inconsistency between profession and practice throughout his life. It is easy to understand how this came about. Had he resigned his few benefices, he would have deprived himself of his support at Oxford. Residence in his parish, on the other hand, would have brought his academic career to an end and taken from him the power to advance such causes as he had at heart. It was inevitable, if unseemly, that Wycliffe, the unsparing critic of those more successful than he in the race for preferment, should cling with greater sense than is relished by his modern admirers to what he could get.

Not that he got very much. It might have been better for his ecclesiastical superiors had they allowed him a larger share. It is possible to believe in Wycliffe's absolute sincerity as a reformer while at the same time suspecting that a plum or two (and the Church had many at her disposal) even as late as the early 1370s might have shut his mouth for ever. The trouble was that no one in authority foresaw the consequences of leaving him unsatisfied; the lengths that he would go were, in fact, impossible to foresee. Certainly there is no excuse for thinking that he would have refused anything he was offered. As it was, a run of disappointments where he could legitimately expect recognition almost certainly helped to manufacture the violent eccentricity and outspokenness of his last decade. He was not deliberately slighted, but he had bad luck. By 1375 he was too sore for his silence to be bought, even if the bishops had realised the need. In any case they preferred coercion.

His first and probably most galling disappointment, one which, it is permissible to believe, had a far-reaching influence upon the evolution of his thought, arose over the headship of a small Oxford college founded between the years 1361 and 1366 by Simon Islip, then archbishop of Canterbury. As originally designed it was to be a mixed society consisting of four monks from Islip's own cathedral priory of Christ Church and eight needy and deserving secular clerks. All part in its government was vested in the monks, one of whom was to hold the office of warden; the seculars, though their interests received statutory protection, were placed quite explicitly upon an inferior footing.

Given the prevailing temper of the university, it was an unfortunate, indeed an unworkable, arrangement. None of the feuds that rent medieval Oxford—and they were many and deep—was more persistent or more acrimonious than that between the secular clerks forming the majority and the members of the regular orders, whether monks or friars, housed in their midst. If few, the latter were much less haphazardly selected, better organised, better disciplined and more powerfully backed. But the *esprit de corps* of each of the many orders was so great, the character of its theological teaching so well marked and traditional to itself, its competitive sense so well developed that an alliance between any two tended to be short-lived. In the great dispute between monks and seculars the friars were with the latter, though their help was not always welcome even when it was used. Some seculars, of whom Wycliffe was ultimately one, dismissed all the orders as equally pernicious, a living denial of the unity of Christ's church. Beside such quarrels as these the occasional clashes between the rowdier elements of town and gown, for all their much-publicised bloodshed, were insignificant.

The proposal to set up a mixed college of monks and seculars in which the latter were subordinated to the former was therefore bound to lead to trouble. From the sequel it has been argued that Islip, himself a secular doctor, was never wholeheartedly in favour of the inclusion of monks in the foundation. If this were true it is difficult to understand why he was induced to adopt a plan which gave them a complete ascendancy in the new college. On the whole, it is more likely that it was a well-meant but ill-considered scheme intended to bring the two unfriendly parties together. Until practical difficulties led Islip to change his mind, he presumably expected the fellows to abide by the statutes he had granted them. These were brought into force in 1363 when on 20 March the archbishop nominated the monk Henry Woodhall first warden of Canterbury College. Harmony was short-lived. By December 1365 Islip had decided to abandon the experiment and to convert his college into a wholly secular one. Woodhall was dismissed in favour of Wycliffe, while three seculars were appointed to take the place of the original monk fellows. Soon afterwards Islip caused new statutes to be drawn up embodying this change of plan. Their validity, however, depended upon their receiving not only the royal assent but also that of Canterbury cathedral priory; before either had been obtained Islip was dead (26 April 1366).

This event left Wycliffe and his three intruded fellows in a decidedly anomalous position. But all might still have been well had not the new archbishop by a rare stroke of ill-fortune been the one monk to attain the primacy of Canterbury between the twelfth century and the sixteenth. They could hope for very little sympathy from Simon Langham, who before his consecration had been abbot of Westminster. It was only to be expected that he would reinstate Woodhall and this he duly did on 22 April 1367. When the seculars in possession ignored his mandate, he took steps to expel them, at the same time cutting off the greater part of their income. Wycliffe and his friends had a hopeless case, but they decided to fight by appealing over the head of the archbishop to the papal court. Meanwhile they seem to have retained possession of the college buildings and a fraction of its revenues. After the usual delays the verdict, as it was almost bound to be, was given against them; and by 1371, if not before, Wycliffe was deprived and back once more in residence at Queen's. The expenses of his unsuccessful lawsuit cannot have been light. It was probably in order to raise money for it that on 12 November 1368 he exchanged his rectory of Fillingham for the much less valuable benefice of Ludgershall in Buckinghamshire. By such an exchange it was possible for a needy clerk to capitalise the difference in income between the living he surrendered and the one he received. The 'chop-church', as such a man was opprobriously named, received a cash payment from the brokers who arranged the transfer. Although frowned upon by most reformers and soon to be roundly condemned by Archbishop Courtenay, these pecuniary transactions were then common.

Wycliffe had suffered both vexation and financial loss

over the affair of Canterbury College. But the legality of
the decision by which he and his fellows were deprived
cannot be questioned. They were neither the victims of a
malicious prosecution nor of a corrupt tribunal, but of
Islip's omissions and their own obstinate litigiousness.
Nevertheless, Wycliffe had become prominently identified
at Oxford with the cause of the seculars and henceforward,
as never publicly before, he was the chief academic enemy
of monasticism. On the other hand, he showed no great
resentment towards the court that had rejected his appeal.
How little cause he had at that time to feel that his deserts
were overlooked by the pope was shown in January 1371
when Gregory XI made him a canon of Lincoln and
promised him a prebend there when a vacancy should
arise.

Wycliffe's reputation was growing steadily, at any rate
within his own order. Unfortunately, it is not yet possible
for us to assign him a place in the history of scholarship—
less because his works have been insufficiently studied
than because it is still necessary to study them in isolation.
Thanks to the zeal of the Wyclif Society most of them
have been printed; but those of his predecessors and contemporaries, in so far as they have survived, still remain
unprinted and therefore virtually forgotten. It is impossible to say how much of Wycliffe's thought was original,
how much derived from his unremembered teachers.
There is enough evidence to show that he was indebted to
the 'Profound Doctor' Thomas Bradwardine for his predestinarianism, to FitzRalph for his theory that only a
ruler in a state of grace deserved authority, though in
each case he gave his borrowings a characteristic twist of
his own. But until the history of fourteenth-century
scholasticism has been written, and more particularly that
of its Oxford masters, Wycliffe's personal contribution to
its growth cannot be assessed. All that can be ventured at
this stage is that he was held in high regard by his
academic contemporaries, that his opponents, however
exasperated, treated him with evident respect, and that, as
the works themselves show, even if his intellectual weapons
were not his own they were wielded with uncommon skill.

The uses he made of them will be considered later. The point in need of emphasis here is that it is far too soon to answer the question: Was Wycliffe a great thinker? We can only guess, though with the knowledge that those better placed than we, even when they abhorred his influence, were willing to concede that he was. A less provisional answer would in any event be out of place in this book.

Nor can Wycliffe's daily life be reconstructed in any but the barest outline. Until 1371 at least it was, we must suppose, fully occupied by study, disputation and teaching within the university. Yet in one of those rare passages of personal reminiscence scattered through his writings, in an open letter composed in his last exile at Lutterworth, he bursts into a rhapsody on the town of Oxford that proves him to have been keenly sensitive to the beauty of its site and of its wooded and watery setting.

Little that he knew exists today. When he perforce turned his back on the town for ever most of the gothic buildings that now remind the visitor of its medieval greatness were not yet begun. They belong to the next two centuries and, because of the architectural conservatism of the university, to even later times. Wycliffe hardly lived to see even the first of the great perpendicular colleges on which a series of episcopal founders lavished their taste and the profits of busy careers in church and realm. For although the foundation-stone of New College had been laid in 1380, it was not until after his death that its first quadrangle was ready for occupation. All Souls and Magdalen belonged to a still more distant future.

If, wandering through the modern city, we ask ourselves what was already there in Wycliffe's day, the sum total is absurdly small. Only two, for example, of the dreaming spires are medieval: St. Mary's and St. Frideswide's (now the cathedral). Of the fifteen churches standing within the walls but two again, St. Michael's-at-the-North-Gate and St. Peter's-in-the-East, survive substantially unchanged. St. Mary's itself was almost wholly rebuilt in the second half of the fifteenth century. A little later still the interior of St. Frideswide's was transformed by the construction of an elaborate stone vault above the presbytery; the chapter house and the Latin chapel alone are much as Wycliffe knew them. Among the colleges then founded, only Merton retains buildings with which he could have been familiar. The choir of its chapel, externally at least (for nothing could be less catholic than the frigid atmosphere within), dates from the 1290s; the last two ranges of 'Mob quad' containing the library were finished in 1379; and the hall, though more than once drastically restored, still preserves something of its thirteenth-century form. Of Wycliffe's Balliol and Queen's there is not a single trace, nor of the Austin friary in which he used to lecture. This last and all the other religious houses, including Rewley and Oseney, have been totally destroyed. The ranges of chambers which survive at Worcester College and the remains of the frater in Christ Church were built after his time.

Among all these changes the three really enduring features of Oxford have been its street-plan, its waterways and the line of its stone walls. From Carfax north and east ran the broad thoroughfares in which the shops clustered and the markets were held and where at times football was played by the younger students. All the other streets, though paved, were narrow; as Oriel Street and the Turl still are. The six gates, which ought to have been closed at night and generally were, are easy even now to identify; and where the walls no longer stand their site can usually be traced.

The townsmen who dwelt within them probably did not number more than five thousand, including women and children. Down to 1300 Oxford had been a prosperous and expanding place of trade. During the succeeding period, thanks partly to general economic causes which affected many inland towns and to the Black Death, but also to the increasing powers exercised by the students, it ceased to grow and even began to decline. Having lost the pre-eminence which its possession of the only market in the neighbourhood had once given it and having seen its hopes as a centre of the weaving industry disappointed, the Oxford of the mid-fourteenth century was becoming increasingly but unhappily dependent upon its university. The two corporations could not live comfortably side by side, and of the two, when it came to a conflict, the academic had, and to be sure deserved, the more influential friends.

The area within the walls was not therefore uncomfortably crowded and as a result of depopulation rents were falling throughout the century. No attempt was made to prevent colleges and other societies from buying up land inside the boundaries of the borough. There was no specifically university quarter; townsmen and scholars dwelt, as they have done ever since, in close proximity. Some districts were, no doubt, more tightly packed than others, but in several we hear of tenements vacant and ruinous, and of open spaces so derelict that they could be used for shows and sports. Even amid the scores of academic halls, the narrow shops around the market, the overhung entries leading to houses, built partly of timber and partly of the local stone, with their courtyards and stables, there was room for an occasional pig-sty and a number of graveyards. And the like tale of decay had to be told about the suburbs that had grown up in better days outside the walls; here, too, there were sites ready for the founders of colleges.

But although Oxford, unlike the great university cities of the continent—Paris, Bologna and Padua—was only a small provincial market-town, and a depressed one at that, it was not entirely remote from the great world. A few miles away was Woodstock, which kings often visited and where princes were born. The upper Thames valley was a rich agricultural region, a land of thriving household knights rather than of great lords. For these busy courtiers Oxford was the natural meeting-place. The university thus enjoyed a degree of contact with the ruler and his entourage which did something to compensate it for its isolation. On the other hand, its distance from the centres of episcopal government meant for its clerks a freedom that they would never have secured in London. Neither remote nor overshadowed it was, in fact, ideally placed, not far from the centre of England and near to many ancient highways. It had already begun to attract its first tourists; we hear of a convalescent knight who was anxious to spend a month or two there, with his esquire and valet, 'to take recreation'. And if all the learning was bad for trade, there was some compensation in the fact that the university drew men not only for higher study but also for more elementary kinds of instruction.

A grammar school was attached to Merton by its founder with a master in charge, to whom even the dons were encouraged to 'have recourse without a blush'. There were as well a number of halls, similar in constitution to the academic halls, where Latin grammar was taught and boys prepared for admission either to the courses of the university or directly to the learned professions. One, at least, in the late fourteenth century, kept by a married master called Thomas Sampson, provided a grounding in accountancy, conveyancing, estate management and business methods. His pupils were also taught how best to compose an idiomatic letter in French or Latin as well as the outlines of polite heraldry. Sampson, to judge from the number of his manuals to survive, must have been the most popular Oxford crammer of his day. In the next century and probably earlier there were others in the town who gave instruction in the elements of the English common law. Besides all these there were the servants and tradesmen, barbers, butlers, manciples and cooks who counted as members of the university and formed a community distinct from their brethren of the town. Such was Wycliffe's Oxford. Though it yet had few noble buildings, it must have drawn both charm and pleasure from its setting. Surrounded by its wooded hills and lazy streams, with the royal forests of Wychwood and Shotover near at hand, it offered its inhabitants many opportunities for those country pursuits, lawful and forbidden, that both townsfolk and scholars loved.

Here in this small, changing and largely youthful world, the governors of which were not venerable heads of houses as in later times but regent masters in their late twenties and early thirties, most of Wycliffe's life was passed. Though he never held important office in the university, he enjoyed enormous prestige—and, what is more, seems to have deserved it. Even his enemies agreed that he was 'the flower of Oxford, in philosophy second to none, without a rival in the discipline of the schools'. From the fact that those who engaged him in controversy cultivated an almost grotesque degree of flattery in their references to him it might be deduced that his self-esteem was excessive and provoked amusement. His own attempts at humour make sad reading. The best that a modern admirer can say of them is that they display an 'elephantine playfulness'. The signs that his head might be easily turned by success were already there.

But the esteem in which he was held is undoubted. One of his staunchest followers has recorded a perhaps not wholly imaginary conversation which he claims to have had with the archbishop of Canterbury in 1407 about his dead leader. In this exchange Thorpe represents himself as saying: 'Sir, Master John Wycliffe was holden of full many men the greatest clerk that they knew then living; and therewith he was named a passing ruly [i.e. virtuous] man and an innocent in his living.' To which Archbishop Arundel, the enemy of all Lollards, replied: 'Wycliffe your author [i.e. founder] was a great clerk and many men held him a perfect liver.' No one of his many detractors ever accused him of incontinence or the lower forms of self-indulgence; pride and disappointed ambition are the charges preferred.'

By 1371 his academic prestige was firmly founded upon a body of philosophical writing, which, whatever its doctrinal implications—and they need never have been made explicit—he strayed no farther from orthodoxy than was normal, inevitable, in the free discussion of the schools. Their Latin debarred them from reaching minds capable of being misled. In all else as in that he had ever shown himself an obedient subject of Holy Church. If his literary achievement was impressive, so too was his personal influence. It is evident from the success with which he was later able to gather about him a group of bright and ambitious young scholars (even though most deserted him when threatened with persecution) that he had the

Chapter Two

The Government and the Church

WYCLIFFE'S political adventures owed much to those under whose patronage he was now in the early 1370s called upon to speak and act. The last years of Edward III's reign form one of the most confused periods in fourteenth-century history. If we ask in whose employment the Oxford master was earning his promotion, the reply that it was the king's, though formally correct, is practically inadequate. For a group, and a far from coherent group, of lay politicians was at this time disposing of the royal power. Much of the significance of Wycliffe's exploits is lost if one does not realise the abnormal conditions under which the government of England was being carried on during the decade of his political activity. It was a period of royal minority, in which the childhood of Richard of Bordeaux immediately followed the second childhood of his grandfather, Edward III. In the only sense that mattered, the country was without a head.

Now, in medieval England the form of government was monarchical and the very first condition of its political health was that the king should rule; rule, of course, according to law and custom and with due regard for the opinion of those whose birth or office entitled them to counsel him, but, above all, rule. His personal initiative and supervision were essential. That being so, a minority offered an insoluble problem. There could be no one with a clear title to exercise the royal authority on behalf of an infant king. Even when there was someone with prestige and experience, an uncle or an elder statesman, it was generally unwise to entrust him with much power. And similar trouble might arise in the case of a king who became a dotard or an invalid, unless his heir was fit for the task. Usually the monarchy was put into commission and a council of the great empowered to act as trustees. But it was an artificial arrangement and rarely worked well for long. Minorities could, in fact, only cease to put an intolerable strain upon the machinery of government when monarchy had become so limited as to be no longer personal.

When a young man Edward III had been as active, if not as assiduous in business, as his grandfather Edward I, but unlike him he wore badly. Soon after his fiftieth birthday (he was born in 1312), he began to lose interest in his work. Although his physical vigour was not so impaired as to prevent him from spending much of his time hunting, his mental grasp and attention to duty gradually slackened. This became more marked after the death of his queen in 1369, and thenceforward he passed much of his time as a recluse in his country manor-houses and hunting-boxes; even his rare visits to the capital were often secret and unconnected with official business. Nor was he satisfied with the pleasures of the chase and of the cellar. As his health declined, he fell more and more under the influence of Alice Perrers, a grasping and unscrupulous woman who had became his mistress by December 1364 and was to stay with him long enough to rob his corpse.

One of the troubles of Edward's dotage was that it was neither sudden nor complete. Had it been so, definite steps to deal with the situation might have been forced upon the baronage. As it was, the king was lazy rather than imbecile. There could be no formal regency; he was still nominally fit to rule, and a crisis might rouse him to brief activity or to a display of that affability which still disarmed criticism. But the necessary driving-force behind government was lacking and confusion was the inevitable result.

The king's withdrawal found the greater offices of state in the control of a group of clerical ministers headed by William Wickham, an able civil servant of humble family who had in 1367 been advanced by royal patronage to the rich see of Winchester. From 1363, if not before, until his dismissal in 1371, Wickham enjoyed a position of rare influence. As the chronicler Froissart put it with little exaggeration, 'everything was done by him and without him nothing was done'. That this could be said of any subject was a measure of the decline of the royal authority since Edward's middle years. It is possible that this state of affairs might have lasted until the end of the reign had England remained at peace. But at the beginning of 1369 the French declared war. A series of English reverses and the prospect of high taxation led to a demand, in which lords and commons joined in the parliament of February 1371, for the removal of the clerical administration and its replacement by laymen more in touch with the country's military needs. The king made no obvious attempt to retain his former servants in office. For the rest of the reign—and Edward survived until 21 June 1377—the direction of affairs, with intermittent and increasingly rare participation by the king, rested in the hands of a council in which lay interests predominated.

In the absence of most of the conciliar records for this period, it is difficult to pin responsibility for the decisions taken upon individuals or groups of councillors. According to hostile chroniclers the ringleader of the opposition to Wickham in 1371 had been the twenty-four-year-old John Hastings, earl of Pembroke, already a soldier of renown, a notorious evil-liver and credited with greedy designs upon the liberties of the church. That his quarrel with Wickham was merely political was shown next year when he appointed the bishop one of his executors. It was more to the point that he was closely associated with Edward, prince of Wales, under whose command he had recently served.

The Black Prince, after a military career which, empty of achievement as it may appear to us, had put him in the forefront of European commanders, was a mortally sick man when after eight years' absence he returned to England in January 1371. His ill-health prevented him from playing for long the rôle in government to which he was entitled by inheritance and personal prestige. But at first, at least, he showed some activity, and right down to his death on 8 June 1376 he was, or was thought to be, a powerful influence behind the scenes. Like most heirs to the throne, he was willing for it to be believed that he shared the country's mistrust of his father's intimates. In fact, he seems to have been on good terms with most of them and must bear considerable responsibility for what was done in 1371 and after. His only living child, the future Richard II, born at Bordeaux in 1367, was not yet out of the nursery. As the prince's health gave way, his place as the old king's deputy was taken by his next surviving brother, John, duke of Lancaster, a rather ambiguous figure who was to hold the stage in a variety of parts for more than another quarter of a century.

Contemporaries differed widely in their estimates of John's character, but at least agreed that it was not colourless. It is significant that foreign observers, untouched by the factiousness of English politics, lean to the more favourable view. This was perhaps because, like his father and brothers, he accepted without question the chivalrous traditions of his order. He was conventional in everything, in his devoutness as much as in his *courtoisie*. Restless, proud and somewhat incautious in his arrogance, enormously wealthy, open-handed and personally magnificent, he was bound to inspire both admiration and mistrust. But if he made enemies, he was successful in drawing within his orbit most of the ablest careerists of his day. Though his achievements as a soldier were more showy than lasting, he had his victories in diplomacy. He preferred an advantageous peace to the chances of war and it would have been better for his father's empire had the English barons shared his insight. Well served he certainly was, and within the limitations of his class and training not without a political dexterity of his own. As a none-too-friendly observer tells us, 'the temporal lords always feared John of Gaunt because of his might, his prudence and his extraordinary ability'. In appearance he was 'a tall spare man, well-knit and erect, as a soldier should be, a man whose conversation was reserved, having something which with an enemy would pass for haughtiness and with a friend for dignity'. His loyalty to his father, his elder brother and afterwards to the young king his nephew was unshakable. Even John Wycliffe, the persecuted heretic, never had any reason to doubt Lancaster's constancy as a friend.

The Black Prince and his brother were the natural leaders of the council during their father's incapacity. But they did not enjoy an unlimited use of the executive power and they were often absent by reason of illness or of business elsewhere. Responsibility was shared with those earls, barons and knights who, along with a few bishops and clerks, made up the body of active councillors. Their main concern was naturally with the conduct of the war, to success in which all else (save private advantage) was vainly subordinated. Its mounting cost—and from the first operations went badly—drove them to plunge blindly into a head-on quarrel with the church. This was no more successful than the French war. When the sound and the fury died down in the inevitable compromise, it was seen that the only lasting sufferers were the heavily taxed clergy and the government's academic champions; it utterly destroyed the ecclesiastical prospects of one rising Oxford theologian. Its responsibility for Wycliffe's worldly ruin makes a brief account of its origins necessary here.

By the reign of Edward III centuries of mutual accommodation had greatly reduced the area of possible dispute between the claims of church and state. There was, for example, little disposition any longer to question the working agreement which had defined the frontiers between the two systems of law. What was called 'benefit of clergy' exempted a clerk from punishment for felony in the royal courts, but for all other purposes he was subject to the law of the land. The layman in his turn was liable to trial in the courts Christian by a bishop or some other judge for a variety of misdeeds (many of them serious) and was obliged to have resort there for the hearing of all matrimonial and testamentary causes. What was more, the royal power was at the disposal of the ecclesiastical judges to enforce their sentences on clerk and layman alike. The church, on its side, was willing to tolerate the right of a lay patron to dispose of the livings in his gift and made no attempt to burden the laity with taxation other than the customary tithes and dues. But although the gap had been partly closed, there was still some room for disagreement. The two great issues over which the battle in Wycliffe's day was fought were the taxation of the clergy and the pope's claim to appoint to the higher offices of the church in England. These defied a peaceful solution precisely because they were of vital strategic importance to both parties. Both were of long standing, but time had done little to weaken their urgency.

Although all Englishmen served two masters, the ones who were most often made aware of their dual dependence were those subjects of the king who were 'the men of Holy Church' *par excellence,* the English clergy; and never more painfully aware than by taxation. They probably numbered rather more than 2 *per cent.* of the total population; that is to say, from fifty to sixty thousand souls. Between them they possessed huge endowments which they owed to the past generosity of pious laymen and which had been increased in value by the good management of successions of clerical landlords. Their property, which may have yielded an income three times that of the king, was not at all evenly divided among them. While the majority of churchmen were little better off than the peasants they lived among, a few, known opprobriously to their critics as 'possessioners'—or, as we might say, capitalists—enjoyed large revenues and kept great state. They, very naturally, were those from whom the taxes were demanded: the bishops and abbots, whose revenues equalled those of the wealthiest laymen; the scores of deans, archdeacons and prebendaries, holding three, four or even more stalls in cathedral and collegiate churches together with at least one well-paid living, who enjoyed stipends that a rich knight might envy.

That these 'possessioners', themselves so much a part of the fabric of contemporary landed society, should have been required to subscribe their quota towards the expenses of government, especially in time of war, was only reasonable. No one likes paying taxes, however convinced he may be that they are needed. What hardened reluctance to meet the king's demands into indignant opposition was that the clergy were exposed to similar pressure from a financially embarrassed pope. The latter, by the exercise of an absolute authority which ecclesiastical law and practice acknowledged to be his, could dispose freely of the property of all churchmen without even needing to obtain their consent. The right to tax belonged to what was called 'the fullness of his power' (*plenitudo potestatis*). Direct papal taxation began in 1199 with a special levy to pay for the Fourth Crusade, but it was not long before this was converted into a series of regular and frequent imposts for the general purpose of the Roman see. The English clergy might, and did, protest that they were being ruined in the interests of a policy that did not concern them; they could not deny the papal right to tax. But if they were powerless, their lay masters were not prepared to allow them to be exploited for the benefit of others. The king could make himself thoroughly unpleasant about the steady flow of English gold overseas; and he could at a pinch stop its export altogether. Nothing but a share of the proceeds could secure his connivance at papal taxation. What that share was to be was matter for constant negotiation. By the reign of Edward II it amounted to 92 *per cent.* of the total yield, or three times the sum that the clergy voted that king direct.

The pope, therefore, was virtually taxing the English clergy for the king's benefit; his own advantage scarcely justified the trouble of collection. It is hardly surprising that with the outbreak of Edward III's war with France the papacy, quite out of sympathy with the objects of royal expenditure, discontinued its taxation. There was no papal tax between the beginning of the war in 1337 and the peace of 1360. That which immediately followed the treaty of Calais was paid to Edward III as a contribution towards the ransom of King John of France; the English clergy, that is to say, were mulcted to relieve the French treasury. When, however, Gregory XI in 1372 decided to revive the practice he did not intend Edward III to benefit at all; it was because he badly needed money himself.

That the English clergy had had no papal tax to pay during the first part of the Hundred Years War did not mean that they had enjoyed a period of unusual immunity. Like their lay brethren, they had been most heavily taxed by the king. The taxation had been screwed out of them in the teeth of rising opposition. The two convocations of Canterbury and York had even offered successful resistance to the king's demands for money. In 1356, for example, a deputation of lay councillors sent to that of the southern province was obliged to content itself with a sixth of what was asked, even though the bishops at least affected to be in favour of something more generous. A crisis might have arisen earlier but for the interval of peace; it was precipitated by the renewal of the war.

In the parliament of June 1369 the commons agreed to an increased duty on exported wool for three years. The prelates, asked to arrange for the grant of an annual tenth from the clergy for the same period, demurred until they had had a chance to consult their inferior brethren who were not in parliament. For some reason, perhaps on account of the plague which raged that summer, it was decided to take soundings in diocesan synods instead of the usual provincial convocations. For the clergy this cumbrous procedure had the advantage of making agreement slow. No grant had been made by the autumn when the king ordered both convocations to be assembled. In that of Canterbury, which met at St. Paul's in London in January and February 1370, no amount of haranguing by the councillors, including John of Gaunt and Archbishop Whittlesey himself, would induce the lesser clergy to agree to the whole of the king's demands. Their offer of two-thirds was rejected by the council. It was only after a fresh appeal that their obstinacy seems at last to have been overcome. This concession, made in response to the rising temper of the laity, came too late to prevent indignation from boiling over in the parliament of the following year. The clerical ministers were its first victims.

At least part of the trouble in 1369–70 had been due to an attempt *to* commit the church to taxation in advance of, even possibly altogether without, the consent of its traditional representatives in convocation; to assert the supremacy of parliament. The prelates had successfully resisted this attack, but it was repeated once more in 1371 by the new government which had driven Wickham and his episcopal colleagues from office. To meet the needs of the army it was thought necessary to raise £100,000 by direct taxation. The commons agreed to make provision for half this amount on the understanding that the church was answerable for the remainder. The bishops and abbots who sat in parliament insisted on referring the matter to the two convocations. This time their reply was unacceptable to the laymen in control and a critical debate followed. It was characteristic of the divisions within the church's own ranks that the ensuing offensive against the 'possessioners', though undoubtedly inspired and throughout maintained by such anti-clerical hotheads as the earl of Pembroke, was noisily supported by ecclesiastics. Those lesser loyalties that bred strife between monks, friars and secular priests at Oxford so far triumphed in 1371 that the laity's spokesmen before parliament were two Austin friars. Like the other mendicant orders, the Austins had long entertained opinions in favour of a return to the simple poverty of the Apostles, which made them feared critics of the 'possessioners', and defied every official attempt to stamp them out.

The record only establishes the identity of one of the two friars: John Bankin, a D.D. from the Oxford house of his order, where Wycliffe was accustomed to lecture. This makes Wycliffe's own presence in the parliament of 1371 the more significant; it may be supposed that he was there to encourage his friends. Though, as far as we know, he remained silent, the views they expressed were at least afterwards his own. Bankin and his unnamed brother put in a brief treatise in which they argued with the usual profuse citation of authorities dear to scholastic disputants that it was justifiable to seize the property of the church for the common good. What pious laymen had given could lawfully be resumed by their heirs in the interests of self-preservation. The prelates were rebuked for having set a bad example of selfishness in a national emergency. It is not surprising that an abbot present took careful note of these hostile propositions. The vigilance of the ecclesiastical authorities had been aroused and henceforward they would be quick to track down and expose these and similar errors. The point of Bankin's argument was equally quickly grasped by his lay audience. For Wycliffe reports having heard one lord declare, 'when war breaks out we must take from the endowed clergy a portion of their temporal possessions as property that belongs to us and in common to the whole kingdom'. Nevertheless, the spiritual peers braved it out; they would only consent to the grant of £50,000 demanded of them if it received the approval of convocation. They did not decline to recommend their inferiors to acquiesce, and with this parliament decided to be content.

The middling clergy, on whom the burden fell most heavily, showed their normal reluctance to vote the desired tax. The convocation of Canterbury province assembled at St. Paul's on 24 April 1371 and held out for a fortnight. It was not until it had met in special session in the presence of the Black Prince and other magnates at the duke of Lancaster's Savoy Palace that on 3 May it yielded to the council's menaces. It agreed to contribute only £40,000, the remaining £10,000 was to be found by the poorer province of York. Such a heavy impost was unprecedented and provoked more than one monastic chronicler to angry lamentation. The hoped-for total was only obtained by squeezing those clergy who were traditionally exempt. Even so, the bishop collectors were still some thousands of pounds in arrears in the autumn of 1372.

Hardly had this enormous sum been granted, and while it was still in process of extraction, when the harassed clergy in April 1372 learnt that they were about to be asked to find another £20,000 to help pay for the wars of Gregory XI in Italy. Their groans achieved some slight alleviation when on 1 July the pope agreed to be content with 100,000 crowns (£15,800) instead, provided that this sum was remitted punctually in two instalments at Easter and Michaelmas 1373. The bishops, had they been left to themselves, would scarcely have ventured to disobey this unwelcome order; but they were spared a painful compliance by the swift intervention of the laity. The government forbade them to levy the subsidy demanded, replied in kind to Gregory's indignant remonstrances and even went so far as to arrest and imprison one of his agents. The clergy were not slow to withhold their contributions once it was clear that responsibility for their inaction had been shouldered by the council. Not a penny reached the papal coffers at Avignon by the dates appointed.

Heartened by this easy victory and evidently believing that Gregory's lack of money would make him amenable to pressure, the councillors were tempted to drive their advantage home on a wider front. They had other grievances which the renewal of the war sharpened. If papal taxation at such a moment seemed intolerable, hardly less so did the pope's claim to fill certain benefices in England, especially when those he nominated were the king's enemies. It has already been noted that the Roman see had consistently refrained from any attempt to impede the lay owner of an advowson in the free exercise of his right of presentation. Since a more aggressive policy here would have achieved nothing but vexation, this restraint was wise. No such self-denial, on the other hand, was necessary in the case of those numerous benefices, including the most valuable, which were in the gift, either by presentation or election, of ecclesiastics.

The medieval bishop possessed, when he was allowed to enjoy it in peace, an extensive patronage. Not only did he present to the many livings with which his see had usually been endowed, but he had as a rule the right to fill the stalls in his cathedral (if it were not a monastery) and often in several other collegiate churches as well. The bishop of Exeter, for example, appointed the canons of Bosham in Sussex and of Glasney in Cornwall in addition to those of Exeter itself; and the four archdeaconries of Exeter, Barnstaple, Totnes and Cornwall could be used by him to advance his kinsmen or his servants to places of rank and wealth. Elsewhere, the bishop of Lincoln had eight archdeaconries at his disposal and the archbishop of

York had five; both had an exceptionally plentiful supply of prebends. Canterbury's cathedral was served by the monks of Christ Church, while its tiny diocese required the ministrations of only a single archdeacon; but the primate had some compensation in being able to select the canons of Wingham and South Malling and no less than eight deans. A good example of his other patronage was the rectory of Mayfield, Sussex, valued for taxation at £60 a year, with which Islip endowed his Oxford college.

Apart from the many rich benefices in the gift of churchmen, there were also those to which churchmen elected. Subject to the rights of king and primate, the duty of choosing a bishop belonged by tradition to the canons or monks of his cathedral church. Deans were normally elected by their chapters, abbots and priors by their monastic houses. Elective benefices therefore included most of the plums for which a clerk might strive, though he could hope to obtain an income which equalled or even surpassed theirs in value by amassing enough smaller morsels of preferment held concurrently. In 1366 before he had become a bishop, but when he was also keeper of Edward III's privy seal and much employed about the court, William Wickham admitted to being in possession of the archdeaconry of Lincoln, eleven canonries and prebends and the Cornish living of Menheniot, which altogether brought him a taxable revenue of £875 *per annum* and, in fact, a good deal more. No benefice on his list was elective; only two, and those nearly the least remunerative, were the property of lay patrons; the rest, though he owed almost all of them to the generosity of his royal master, belonged in the ordinary course to his fellow-churchmen.

While Wickham's case was one of uncommonly successful acquisitiveness, it well illustrates the superior value of ecclesiastical patronage over that owned by laymen. It is also an excellent example of the way in which appointments normally at the disposal of a prelate could sometimes be made by the crown. When a bishop died or vacated his office, the lands and other temporal possessions of his see were taken into the custody of his feudal superior, the king, and administered to the royal profit until restored to his successor. By English law an advowson was such a temporality, and long before the reign of Edward III this rule had been applied in a way highly profitable to the crown to include the filling of stalls and cathedral dignities as well as of the rectories in the bishop's gift. Further, this extension of the right of *regale*, as it was called, had been fully, if reluctantly, accepted in practice by pope and church. It was by its exercise that Wickham became archdeacon of Lincoln on 26 April 1363; for Bishop Ginewell had died on 5 August 1362 and the temporalities remained in the king's hands until they were granted to his successor Buckingham on the following 23 June.

Once the bishop was in occupation, however, the crown had no direct say in these appointments. The king could ask that a prebend should be given to a servant, and his wishes carried weight, but as often as not he was rebuffed. In the case of bishoprics, on the other hand, where the right of election lay with the cathedral chapter or monastery, his assent had to be sought and the temporalities would remain in his custody at least until it was given. Otherwise the church retained control of all its principal appointments. Nevertheless, this was far from meaning that electors elected or that bishops and others exercised their freedom of choice without interference from above; only that the chief threat to their independence came not from the royal but from the papal court. The king might threaten and coerce, but the pope could legally command. Here again, as in the matter of taxation, the *plenitudo potestatis* was used to justify any amount of activity by the Holy See, entitling the pope to treat as his own all benefices in his subjects' gift, whether elective or not. He was, as he frequently remarked in his official letters, 'the universal pastor of all churches', and the actual occupants were his creatures. That he did not, in fact, choose to take all ecclesiastical appointments wholly into his own hands was to be regarded as evidence of his benevolent moderation. His power was absolute—in theory. In practice, its exercise was restricted to the filling of those benefices which he cared to 'reserve' for himself. He could, and often did, make special reservations of particular benefices; in Edward III's time nearly all bishoprics were thus reserved and the pope 'provided' his nominees to them at every vacancy. In addition, certain types of vacancy were subject to a general reservation. These tended to increase steadily in number, and during the early fourteenth century several new classes were created. Thus all benefices vacated by persons at the Roman court or within two days' journey of it, as a result of death, promotion, deprivation or resignation, all benefices vacated by papal officials from the cardinals down to the scribes in the chancery, and all benefices vacated anywhere in consequence of a papal order were automatically reserved.

The motives for this centralising policy were largely financial. The chosen recipient of a papal provision owed his benefactor a not insignificant slice of his first year's receipts. These annates, as they were generally called, were an important item in the papal budget. Again, the government of the Roman church called for the services of a large body of highly-trained and whole-time administrators, the payment of whom put a heavy strain on the resources of the Holy See. This could only be relieved by promoting members of the clerical staff to stalls and churches throughout Western Christendom. What may have begun under pressure of necessity was without doubt continued and expanded for less creditable reasons. The princely incomes drawn by certain favoured cardinals, usually the pope's own kinsmen, from a score of valuable benefices which they never visited in person, were a just cause of scandal. The same mixture of good and bad motives can be seen at work in the king's use of his patronage to support and reward his civil servants. Neither state nor church found it a simple matter to finance its policy out of income. It is easier to condemn the abuses of the system than to suggest a workable alternative solution to difficulties that were genuine enough.

It would be especially wrong to accept the impression, given much exaggerated currency by polemical writers of that day, that the papal right of provision was employed merely to endow the Roman secretariat at the expense of the provincial churches. The vast majority of English benefices (including all but one of the bishoprics) reserved by John XXII and his successors at Avignon were given to natives who, if they did not live in their cures, at least resided on this side of the channel: royal ministers and servants, men of good birth and education whom the pope considered deserving of promotion, eminent scholars like Wycliffe, lawyers and administrators active in the provincial and diocesan business of the English church. It would not be difficult to show that the court of Rome used its powers as well as, if not indeed a good deal better than, the patrons whom it superseded; for where its own material interests were not primarily at stake, it was capable of applying higher and more consistent standards than any but the best of those on the spot. Centralisation was in part in the interests of efficiency. As long as papal provisions diluted those chosen locally, there was less chance that a chapter would be swamped with kinsmen; and the excessive influence of the local landed families was also kept in check. Perhaps nothing did more to maintain the health of the church than the fact that its bishops were selected neither by pope nor king nor chapter alone, but by a series of involved and sometimes unedifying compromises between the wishes of all three. And, however heated the partisans might at times become, the will to compromise was rarely absent for long. Actions belied words. Unfortunately, historians often show a writer's preference for the latter. It will be a false picture that is derived from the intemperate outbursts of professional advocates alone.

Before 1371 there had been much English criticism of the workings of the system of provision. But the gulf was wide between the anti-papalist case as set out in a succession of parliamentary petitions, beginning with one at Carlisle in 1307 and embodied in such famous legislation as the statutes of Provisors (1351) and Premunire (1353) on the one hand and the policy actually enforced by the government on the other. The king did not discourage the attack on provisions; it might always prove useful and could be employed to strengthen his hands when bargaining with Rome; but Edward III, at least, was perfectly willing to sell out to the popes if the latter made it worth his while. They usually did, by consulting his wishes before making all important appointments and by regularly granting a proportion of all reserved benefices to his servants. As far as Edward III was concerned, a deal with the papacy was always on the cards provided the terms suited him; only he was determined to protect his rights. It would be possible to illustrate the workings of this bargaining policy by scores of examples throughout his long reign. On the whole, he had no cause to regret his willingness to compromise. He enjoyed his share of the provisions and found it easier to square the pope than to cajole or bully the local chapters. King and pope in alliance bade fair to override the freedom of electors and to dispose of most of the churchmen's patronage. The opposition to provision came from other sources than the court, from the English landed classes and to a lesser extent from the clergy themselves, none of whom had the same ease of access to the papal ear as the king and the highest nobility enjoyed.

A letter, drawn up in parliament for despatch to Pope Clement VI on 18 May 1343, sets out the attitude of the malcontents very clearly. The language was perfectly respectful, indeed almost servile, a useful reminder that the devout laity were far from wishing to question the divine authority of the pope; they merely wished to protest against its misuse. The church in England owed its vast endowments, Clement was told by 'his humble and loyal sons, the princes, dukes, earls, barons, knights, citizens, burgesses and all the commons of the realm', to the pious liberality of their ancestors and of themselves. The purposes for which these gifts had been made were in order that 'the services of God and the Christian faith might be honoured, increased and embellished, hospitalities and alms given and maintained, churches and buildings honestly preserved and kept, devout prayers in the same places offered up for founders, poor parishioners aided and comforted and in confession and otherwise fully taught and indoctrinated in their mother tongue by those that had the cure of souls'. And the dangers that followed from the neglect of these were then briefly outlined.

It would be unwise to take all this quite at its face value. A glance at the kinds of men who received their preferment at the hands of lay patrons is not encouraging to those who wish to hear in this letter the first growl of English puritanism. Among them will be found negligent pluralists and absentees, favoured kinsmen and household clerks far busier about their worldly affairs than their parochial duties. Had the laity confiscated the church-men's patronage, it is by no means certain that standards would have risen. The keenest sentiment behind the agitation was without any serious doubt the belief that provision was an offence against the proprietary rights of laymen over the churches their ancestors had endowed. To this, patriotism now came as a reinforcement. The thought that the proceeds of their fathers' generosity went into the pockets of strangers had never been agreeable. When into the bargain these strangers were enemy aliens, French cardinals, giving comfort and succour to the Valois, it was not to be endured. Yet it must not be supposed that more religious feelings were left unstirred by the neglect of a founder's objects in making his benefactions, especially the prayers for the repose of his soul and the souls of his family after death.

The first steps towards reformation were thus taken by men whose consciousness of abuses was sharpest when they were deprived of the ability to commit them themselves. The motives of the lay protestants were a thoroughly human compound of nationalist sentiment and puritanical cen-soriousness not untinged with envy and blatant self-interest. Needless to say, their clerical friends, who stood to gain from their success, were wholeheartedly behind them. The clearest statement of this is to be found in the chronicle of Adam Murimuth (1275?–1347). Murimuth, a squire's son from the upper Thames valley, an Oxford doctor of law who had practised successfully in the Roman courts, the vicar-general and official of the archbishop of Canterbury and a canon of St. Paul's, had every opportunity to know his world. His observations have therefore none of the backwater parochialism of the average monastic annalist. It is interesting to find that he treats a long series of provisions to bishoprics as scandalous and quotes every protest with acclamation. His outspoken and unsparing criticism of papal policy justifies the belief that others of his class thought like him. But the clergy could not easily deny the absolute authority of the Vicar of Christ, and for that reason the brunt of the attack fell perforce to the lot of their lay kinsfolk.

It is only too obvious that Edward III's occasional support for the anti-papalist agitation was deliberately calculated to raise the price of his connivance in the policy attacked, that it was little more than diplomatic blackmail. Indeed, all along the popes seem to have realised that they had nothing to fear from him. Edward's numerous petitions to Avignon for fresh provisions for his servants at the very height of the conflict were sufficient proof of that. The English government was not serious and the Roman court knew it.

So popular indignation remained unassuaged. In 1351 it achieved an apparent victory in the first statute of Provisors, which ordered all elections and presentations to benefices to be free and declared all provision illegal. This 'memorable statute' (as it has been erroneously called) was of little practical effect. Edward III did not cease to take full advantage of his access to the pope's ear and to bargain as before for as large a share in the unabated distribution of English benefices from Avignon. Disputes over particular provisions which he did not like continued to arise from time to time, and individuals who dared to appeal from royal judgements to the court of Rome were called to account and sometimes punished. When two bishops, Thomas Lisle of Ely and William Lynn of Chichester, attempted to use Avignon as a court of appeal from Westminster they were severely treated. In 1365 Edward himself invited parliament to re-enact all the earlier anti-papal legislation, including the statute of Provisors. As usual, this was only meant as a threat, a demonstration of what was in store for those who tried the king too far. It marked no break, for example, in the run of papal provisions to bishoprics, some of which were still made without giving the king the chance to express his views. Thus Whittlesey was provided to Canterbury in 1368 before Edward even knew that the primacy was vacant.

But the legislation of 1365 did lead to the raising of one new issue. For it caused the Holy See to retaliate with a polite reminder that the tribute that King John had promised when he submitted to Innocent III in 1213 had long been in arrears. Prompt payment was requested. This invited and received from parliament the famous if obvious retort that John had had no right to commit his subjects without their consent. All the estates, including the prelates, unanimously and with a finality which it was for once useless to question repudiated the papal claim to the feudal overlordship of England. Only the lay case against provisions went by default so long as the government chose to remain inactive. In 1373 the new men controlling policy, egged on by their supporters in the commons, decided to try the effect of more energetic measures.

The most obvious move, it might have been thought, would have been to order the enforcement of the not inadequate legislation of the previous years. The councillors preferred to begin direct negotiation with Gregory XI. This did not necessarily mean that they were half-hearted—though, as events were to show, some of them had little fight—as over-sanguine. They rated their chances too high. In any case it was useful to have the statutes in reserve if it should come to bargaining. The pope, though bitterly incensed by the treatment of his request for money, agreed to suspend all proceedings against the king's servants in his court until the arrival of an English embassy.

This reached Avignon in September 1373, headed by the Dominican John Gilbert, whom Gregory had recently provided to the see of Bangor. The demands it presented may be summarised under four heads:

(1) that no more appeals should be entertained by the

pope which interfered with the king's exercise of his right of *regale*;

(2) that because travel was dangerous in time of war no Englishman should be cited to appear in person at the Roman court to answer an appeal;

(3) that in order to restore freedom of patronage and election the pope should in future abstain from all reservations and provisions; those already made but not yet carried out should be cancelled; and

(4) that, since the clergy were unable to afford papal taxes as long as the war lasted, the pope should abandon his proposed levy until the restoration of peace.

If Gregory found these requests exorbitant, his poverty was such that he was willing to offer some concessions. As a result, on 21 December an interim agreement was negotiated which allowed time for a fuller discussion of the main points at issue. Gregory promised to postpone for six months the hearing of all cases which touched the right of *regale*, on the understanding that the king would do the same and refrain from disturbing those already in possession of a benefice as the result of a papal provision. Appearance in person at the Roman court was dispensed with for a year; if during the interval fresh disputes arose in the course of which one party asked for a personal citation of his opponent, Gregory undertook to commit the trial to a place in the Low Countries safely accessible from England. Edward III's advisers ratified his side of this agreement on 11 March 1374 and announced that his ambassadors would be ready to meet the pope's at either Calais or Bruges towards the end of June. They had less reason than Gregory to congratulate themselves on the result of Gilbert's mission. Although the Holy See had not refused to negotiate, it had made no surrender of principle. By agreeing to a moratorium for appeals it had avoided any suggestion of intransigence, but it had neither abated its demand for a clerical tax nor shown any willingness to forgo provisions. That it would concede anything substantial on these two crucial points was hardly to be expected. In spite of this the English government persevered with its diplomacy.

In this it was only meeting the wishes of its following in the country, who had displayed some impatience at the lack of practical result from its policy even while Gilbert and his fellows were still at Avignon. In the parliament of October 1373 the commons once again forcibly expressed their abhorrence at the continuation of provisions. For the moment they were met by a reminder that negotiations were in train and a promise that a black-list of all aliens in enjoyment of English benefices should be compiled. Meanwhile, the clergy continued restive. When in December 1373 the convocation of Canterbury, with much grumbling at their 'intolerable yoke', agreed to vote the king his expected subsidy, William Courtenay, the vigorous young bishop of Hereford, put himself at the head of the discontented who numbered the papacy among their oppressors. Neither he nor the clergy of his diocese, Courtenay declared, would give a penny until the king had found a remedy for those mischiefs from which churchmen had suffered long enough. Though it was far from clear what precisely he was complaining of apart from taxation, it is evident that the king's council was under fire from clergy and laity alike. With nothing to show for its conduct of the war but a series of expensive failures, and with divisions and corruption increasing at home, the government badly needed a diplomatic success to restore its waning popularity. On 1 May 1374 the pope selected Bruges as the venue of the conference and appointed his envoys. It was not until 26 July, after the delays seemingly inseparable from medieval diplomacy, that seven English ambassadors received their authority to treat. They must already have been chosen and briefed, since they were able to set out on the morrow for Flanders. Once again they were led by the bishop of Bangor, but this time Wycliffe was of their number, ranking next below Gilbert, as befitted a doctor of theology.

Chapter Three

Wycliffe in Politics, 1371–8

WYCLIFFE'S entry into public life came therefore at a critical and exceptional time. Those who made use of him, instead of following the cautious, well-tried policy of give-and-take laid down by that most successful opportunist Edward III, thought that they could achieve more by being stiff-necked. The king had considered his own interests; they were perhaps more thoughtful of the interests of their class. So for once, if only for a short time, the government helped to whip up rather than to moderate popular exasperation with the endless demands of the Roman church. Coming to the royal service after the anti-clerical victory of 1371, Wycliffe learnt a dangerous lesson. He was by nature intemperate; now he was encouraged to think that he would best please his employers by fighting their battles with all the weapons at his command. He became a partisan when guerrillas were wanted, without seeing that in the long run most statesmen prefer compromise to the fruitless heroism of the last ditch. At any other time he might never have been tempted to his ruin.

It is by no means certain who was responsible for the decision to employ him. The answer usually favoured, namely John of Gaunt, is plausible, but it is just as likely to have been Gaunt's elder brother. Later, the Black Prince's widow was to afford Wycliffe at least as much help and protection as Lancaster, while her household, inherited from her husband, is known to have contained more than one knight who was justifiably suspect of befriending heretics. Nor was Prince Edward wholly free from the warrior's contempt for clerks. There is evidence that he was an outspoken and irascible enemy of those churchmen, including Archbishop Whittlesey, whom he suspected of a reluctance to help pay for the war; and he presided over an assembly in which Wycliffe's anti-papalist arguments were either anticipated or echoed. He did not disagree with the popular outcry of the 1370s and, unlike his brother Lancaster, he was not associated with its betrayal in favour of a truce with Rome in 1375. It may well have been he who diverted the flood of Wycliffe's energy and learning into new channels. He did not live to see the bursting of the banks.

The treatise *On the Incarnation of the Word*, completed about 1370, was the last composition from the scholar's pen that was not deliberately polemical. It has been described with some exaggeration as 'a piece of great religious writing' and as 'a measure of the sacrifice made when the divine became the reformer'. It was certainly his farewell to academic peace. That it involved him in controversy with John Kenningham, an Oxford master from the Carmelite friary at Ipswich, cannot have disturbed him; that was just part of the routine of the schools. Henceforward, however, his books had a more practical intention. At first he aimed only at providing a theoretical case for his employers' desire to coerce and despoil the higher clergy. Later, when this had brought down ecclesiastical censures on his head, he chose to fight back and, deserted by almost all his lay supporters, struck savagely at the very roots of Catholic doctrine in an attempt to confound his accusers. It would be a blunder to suppose that the course of his campaign had been thought out in advance. Like most touchy and passionate controversialists, Wycliffe did not pause to realise where the debate was carrying him.

What was wanted of him in the early 1370s was a reply to the clerical argument that, because the authority of the church was superior to that wielded by the state, it followed that its property should be kept inviolate from all secular uses. The two Austins had sketched an answer in the 1371 parliament and had tried to meet as shortly as possible the more obvious objections that would be raised to the proposal to conscribe the church's wealth in time of war. The occasion was not one for prolonged debate. To argue the secular case at length with all the learning he could command was Wycliffe's subsequent task, and one for which his great eminence as a dialectician specially fitted him. It is not possible to date exactly the moment at which he began work, though his presence as a spectator in the 1371 parliament seems to imply an awakened interest in the subject. A casual remark in a lecture delivered soon after he had taken his doctorate proves that he was already willing to favour his audience with his views on the nature of 'lordship', to the writing up of which he was to devote much of the next five years. Nor was it long after this that he was having to deal with the first criticisms of those whom the Benedictine abbots put up to refute him. All the signs point to 1370 or 1371 as the year in which he first indulged a taste for political controversy.

Lordship over men, as all thinkers agreed, was of divine origin. There was, nevertheless, room for a difference of opinion about the channel by which it was transmitted to rulers from God. According to what may be called the ultramontane theory, as set out for example in the writings of the extreme papalist, Giles of Rome, who flourished about 1300, lordship was only just when it was derived from the Roman church, which had been entrusted with universal dominion over all temporal things and persons; any other authority, such as that possessed by heathen or sinful rulers, could not be acceptable to God and was therefore unlawful. Although Giles's prestige as a thinker deservedly remained great, a succession of hardly less influential scholars declined to adopt his uncompromising position. For some of them at least lordship depended less on the mediation of the church, though that might be desirable for perfect justice, than on the fact that its possessor was in a state of grace. Mortal sin, it was held, automatically deprived a man of true lordship, for the enjoyment of which grace was an indispensable condition.

As first developed, this thesis was applied only to temporal lordship; but it was not long before its scope was extended to include the authority wielded by spiritual persons. If grace was essential in a lay ruler, those holding ecclesiastical office could hardly need it less. The first theologian to take this line and to make it the basis for an attack upon those churchmen who from mortal sin had forfeited their right to lordship was almost certainly Richard FitzRalph, from 1348 to his death in 1360 archbishop of Armagh. FitzRalph in his younger days had been a prominent Oxford theologian who had begun his career with a fellowship at Balliol. But his great book, *On the Poverty of the Saviour,* in which a discussion of lordship was somewhat awkwardly combined with a lively attack upon the mendicant orders, was not published until well after Wycliffe's first residence at the university. A copy presented by its author seems to have reached the library of Merton College in 1356, the year in which Wycliffe was a fellow there. How much the young scholar owed to it is abundantly proved by the close verbal correspondence between it and various passages in his own works.

FitzRalph for some reason failed to make explicit the connection, which obviously existed in his own mind, between the theory of lordship and grace on the one hand and the abuses for which he castigated the friars on the other. When Wycliffe needed a stick to beat not the friars but ecclesiastical possessioners in general, he took over and elaborated FitzRalph's implied argument. But whereas the archbishop had been trying to persuade Pope Clement VI to deprive the friars of their misused privileges, Wycliffe inevitably looked to the laity, and most of all to the English government, to become the instruments of reform. It was therefore necessary for him to reverse the ultramontane view of the relations between church and state and to supply a theoretical justification for the action of the lay power.

This he found, as the imperial champion Marsiglio of Padua had done before him, in some rather strained deductions from the fact of the Incarnation. The priest represented Christ's humanity, the prince His divinity; it followed that the prince was above human laws and that the task of correcting the church's faults within his realm belonged of right to him. This argument in the form we now have it dates from about 1379, but there can be no doubt that it had been stated, though possibly only in spoken disputation, some six or seven years before. For it clearly lies behind an imperfectly reported controversy in which Wycliffe was engaged by two Benedictine opponents in 1372–3. Both parties later wrote up their arguments for publication.

The first and more redoubtable of Wycliffe's adversaries was Ughtred Boldon, a Durham monk who had taken his D.D. at Oxford as long ago as 1357; of the other, Dr. William Binham from St. Albans, less is known, save that he was more nearly Wycliffe's contemporary in the schools. Both outlived him by many years and were permitted to die in the knowledge that their cause had triumphed even in their old university. It is likely that they had been set on to challenge Wycliffe's teaching by their provincial superiors, who met in the triennial chapter of their order at Northampton in September 1372. If so, this vigilance on the part of the Black Monks was the first result of the appearance of Wycliffe's Austin friends in the parliament of the previous year.

How contemporaries judged these learned exchanges is not known. In the middle of them Boldon was called away to become a member of Bishop Gilbert's mission to Avignon. The fact that he should have been chosen to put the English government's case may at first sight seem incongruous. The crown did not necessarily choose its agents on the strength of their opinions, but rather on its estimate of their diplomatic capacity. Boldon, doubtless, like any other envoy, had his detailed instructions and spoke to his brief. There is, in fact, no need to suppose that he was out of sympathy with the policy he was made to serve. There were not many Englishmen who did not wish to see less papal taxation and fewer aliens promoted to benefices within the realm. Yet when Wycliffe rather than Boldon was nominated as Gilbert's only theological assistant at the Bruges conference, it is difficult not to see in this a recognition of his greater suitability as a champion of the lay power. It is noteworthy that most of his colleagues were the political associates of the men in office.

His own connection with them was neither recent nor unrecognised. Already, before he had taken his doctor's degree, he had been teased by Brother John Kenningham with having 'the house of Herod' to guide him. This has generally been interpreted as a scarcely veiled reference to the king's favour, and it can be nothing else. Shortly afterwards, Wycliffe is found describing himself as 'in a special sense the king's clerk', a direct indication of his recruitment to that cadre of royal servants designed for high office. Its first tangible result was his presentation on 7 April 1374 to the rectory of Lutterworth. Having no papal dispensation to hold two such livings in plurality, he relinquished that of Ludgershall soon afterwards. The exchange was a profitable one, since Lutterworth, equal in value to Fillingham, was worth three times as much as Ludgershall. It mattered little to an absentee that it was not so near Oxford. Were it not for Wycliffe's later scorn for the 'Cæsarean clergy', by which he meant those churchmen who neglected their cure of souls to do the king's worldly business, it would not be at all incongruous to find him thus rewarded.

The mission to Bruges cannot be regarded as an outstanding success for English diplomacy, but no detailed account of the negotiations has survived. Wycliffe was absent from England from 27 July to 14 September 1374 and drew some £60 in wages and expenses. What impression he made we can only guess, though it is probably significant that while he remained for some years more a servant useful to the crown, he was never again chosen for diplomatic work. Evidently his uses as a propagandist were greater than as a negotiator. His reputation with his modern admirers has not suffered on this account, since it relieves him from any responsibility for the final settlement. When this was reached at Bruges and proved an almost complete triumph for papal diplomacy he was no longer present. But the deduction that he would never have consented to anything so shameful is devoid of substance; he was an agent, not an initiator of policy. In spite of some popular feeling to the contrary, those in charge of the English government were not prepared to break off negotiations and to declare open war.

To explain why the brave words of 1371–3 were so quickly eaten would need a more extensive knowledge of the council's discussions than its scanty records allow. The break with tradition was probably less great than some extremists like Pembroke had wished. By 1375 Pembroke was dead, the Black Prince was dying and the leadership in the council and in the king's favour had passed to the duke of Lancaster, whose politic character and international outlook disposed him to moderation where the papacy was involved. The illnesses of his father and of his elder brother opened up the prospect of a long minority, with its attendant domestic evils. In addition, an unbroken series of military disasters seems to have convinced the duke that what remained of the English conquests in France had better be stabilised by a truce, thus leaving the future Richard II as well-placed as possible for continuing the war when he came of age. From 24 March 1375 onwards Lancaster was at Bruges in personal charge both of the peace negotiations with the French and of an attempt to seal a concordat with Gregory XI. He cannot be blamed for thinking that a settlement of outstanding disputes with the papacy would help to achieve the still more necessary truce. By the end of the following June agreement had been reached under both heads.

By the concordat, which was set out in six bulls dated 1 September 1375, Pope Gregory went a short way towards satisfying the more pressing claims of the English government. He confirmed all clerks appointed by the crown in possession of their benefices, even where these had been specifically reserved by him for his own disposal. Nine royal nominees whose titles had been disputed by papal candidates in the Roman court were to be molested no more; all benefices reserved by the popes since 1362 which had not actually been enjoyed were set free, and those who had obtained them by ordinary presentation were relieved from the need to pay first-fruits to Avignon; English clerks cited to appear before the papal judges were to be summoned to Bruges or some convenient place in its neighbourhood until peace with France should be achieved or for three years at most if it were not; finally, an investigation was ordered into alleged cases of ruinous neglect by the cardinals of their English churches.

These concessions, by providing remedies for outstanding ills, did something to liquidate the past, but it is obvious how little they did to avoid future trouble. Gregory XI kept himself free to continue the practices that had aroused so much English resentment. Even so, these accommodations cost money. In return for them Gregory accepted £10,000, which came, not out of the king's pocket, but as a matter of course from the long-suffering English clergy. It was agreed that before June 1376 he should be allowed to collect three-fifths of the subsidy he had demanded earlier and that the balance should be paid to him at the termination of the war with France. It was not long before the bishops were being plagued to hurry on the collection in their dioceses. That some were reluctant and dilatory was to be expected.

This virtual surrender did not pass without criticism from the spokesmen of the lay interest at home. It was, to be sure, not the only part of the government's recent handling of affairs that had aroused vindictive feelings in the country. When the 'Good Parliament' gathered at Westminster on 28 April 1376 it was its obvious intention to strike at Lancaster through his associates and to condemn almost every aspect of his policy. Although the most spectacular of the proceedings was the impeachment of various persons about the king for corruption and mismanagement, ecclesiastical questions were not neglected. Two great bills of petitions sent forward by the commons grumbled bitterly at all the old abuses under which the national church continued to suffer, and demanded instant remedy. Some of their phrases echoed earlier protests, but never had the language of complaint been more violent against the traffic in benefices by those 'who dwell in the sinful city of Avignon', against the exactions, the luxury and the corrupting influence of the papal agents or against the alien absentees, whose existence was more injurious to holy church than 'all the Jews and Saracens in the world'. Only the pope himself was spared; the commons preferred to think him the victim of a rotten system. The government's reply to this onslaught was more evasive than truthful. Complainants were reminded that there was already enough legislation on the statute roll to provide an adequate remedy for the abuses named and were led to believe that negotiations on the desired lines were still proceeding. With that the commons, having many other things to do, were successfully fobbed off.

To Wycliffe, writing hard at Oxford in favour of the active interference of the lay ruler to deprive sinful clerks of their endowments, the Good Parliament's terminology may have seemed crude, but the ends sought were identical with his own. Since he had returned from Bruges to his room in Queen's he had been labouring at a great pair of treatises into which he packed all his considered thoughts on the subject of dominion. Published by instalments, they were not completed until 1378. As the destructive character of his teaching became apparent, it once more engaged the attention of his Benedictine opponents. In 1375 the provincial chapter of the order met again and at it a number of theologians were chosen to speak publicly at Oxford against him. But soon afterwards one of them, by name John Ayscliffe of Durham priory, was enjoined to silence by his superior on the ground that the task was too hazardous. The reasons given were the great unpopularity of the possessioners and the fact that leading members of the king's council had definitely forbidden Ayscliffe to take part in any activity in the schools likely to lead to schism or disturbance. A number of letters that then passed between the abbots of the order disclosed the extent of their concern. On the wise advice of Thomas de la Mare of St. Albans, a shrewd and experienced statesman, a waiting policy was adopted. With more rope Wycliffe might well hang himself. For the monks to counter-attack in 1375 would only have revealed how powerful were his backers. As it was, these did very little for him. The only benefice procured for him from the government was the rectory of Lutterworth. He was neither made free of the immense ecclesiastical patronage which individual lords of the council controlled nor effectively pressed upon the notice of the Roman church. Yet it would be hard to assert that he wanted nothing. This is belied by the story of the Lincoln prebend, if not also by his reported candidature for the see of Worcester.

Gregory XI's promise of a Lincoln prebend made in January 1371 was repeated in December 1373. When, however, in mid-1375 the well-endowed prebend of Caistor at Lincoln fell vacant, the pope granted it to the illegitimate son of Sir John Thornbury, an English mercenary captain in his service in Italy. There is reason for believing that the young Thornbury stood higher on Gregory's waiting-list than Wycliffe, but the latter took his defeat with a bad grace. That he, a prominent and deserving scholar, should have been passed over in favour of an immature stripling from overseas who had no intention of residing in England, was an insult that rankled. Understandable as such feelings were, they showed little appreciation of the pope's difficulty in satisfying the importunate demands of a thousand clients. Delay and disappointment were the lot of the majority and, rather by accident than by design, the least deserving were often the most successful. Wycliffe, as a result of this affair, began to harbour a sense of persecution. Already, a year or two earlier, he had accused an English critic of wishing to deprive him of his benefices by maligning him at the papal court. Premature though his fears may then have been, it was not long before Gregory's attention was drawn to the objectionable nature of his views. Once the pope's suspicions were aroused, enough errors were found to put an end at length to all Wycliffe's hopes of promotion at his hands. The promise of 1371 was never fulfilled.

His detractors later said that Wycliffe's heresies 'had their origin in his disappointed hope of obtaining the bishopric of Worcester'. The source quoted for this tale was the conversation of Robert Hallam, bishop of Salisbury from 1408 to his death in 1417, and the leading

English advocate of the reform of the church at the momentous Council of Constance. If any opponent of heretics can be regarded as a trustworthy witness against them it is Hallam. His insinuation (if he was its author) need not be believed; it certainly cannot be buttressed by any other evidence, but it is at least credible. The mention of a particular see, moreover one which was vacant in the years when Wycliffe stood a chance of being preferred, may be thought to lend it colour.

Worcester was without its pastor between the death of Bishop Lynn on 18 November 1373 and the provision of his successor on 12 September 1375. It remained vacant, that is to say, until the three-year estrangement between Gregory XI and the English government was healed at Bruges. During this period the wishes of the king's advisers with regard to the provision of bishops were steadily ignored. Rochester, Ely and York went to unofficial candidates, while Worcester and Canterbury were not filled at all. On Lynn's death the monks elected their prior Walter Legh to succeed him. The fact that their choice was formally endorsed by the crown does not necessarily throw any light on the government's intentions. It was quite usual for Edward III to send the electors word of his approval while urging the claims of another clerk upon the pope. In this case we do not know whom the council wanted. It would not be surprising if it was the king's clerk and envoy, Master John Wycliffe.

Legh, the Worcester monk, was precisely the type of bishop-elect who rarely achieved consecration. Nor did he in the distribution of sees which marked the end of hostilities between Westminster and Avignon. The primacy went on 4 May 1375 to Simon Sudbury, and on 12 September following, London, Worcester and Hereford were given new bishops. Legh's supplanter was Henry Wakefield, a clerk of the royal household, whom the council had vainly pressed upon Gregory for Ely two years before. Finally, on 12 October, the keeper of the duke of Lancaster's private seal, Ralph Erghum, was rewarded wth the see of Salisbury. With the possible exception of the new bishop of London, William Courtenay, whose abilities and connections made him an obvious case for promotion, each of these was *persona grata* with the men then acting for the king. Three of them, like Wycliffe, had been among the English ambassadors at Bruges. He had some justification for thinking himself passed over, but how much we may never know. His next employment showed that he was far from having lost his utility to his lay masters, though it added the English hierarchy to the list of his clerical enemies and made his chances of promotion in the church still more remote.

The man who was generally believed to have been behind the Good Parliament's attack on the corrupt and incompetent advisers of the crown was William Wickham, the fallen minister of 1371. His appearance in the rôle of Satan rebuking sin proves that his own record in office was in danger of being forgotten. He had certainly prevented one of the accused, lord Latimer, from being given time to take legal counsel and to arrange his defence. That he was regarded by Lancaster as chiefly responsible for the trial and discomfiture of the latter's friends is shown by the malice with which he was persecuted once the dismissal of parliament had restored the duke's freedom. A great council was called on 13 October 1376 and endured for nearly two months, during which the acts of the Good Parliament were annulled and Wickham was put on trial. The charges against him were based on his conduct as minister before 1371. Although there is no reason to doubt that his actions had sometimes been high-handed and by modern standards dishonest, they do not seem to have been out of the common for his time. In any case, the fact that no action was taken until five years had elapsed justifies a suspicion of the good faith of his accusers. The truth was that Wickham had given offence by becoming once more politically formidable, and the intention was to show that he was morally no better than those who had supplanted him. His condemnation was followed by the seizure of his temporalities in payment of a gigantic fine; only his tonsure saved him from bodily confinement.

In this unsavoury affair Wycliffe played his part. It was

the first occasion in his career when he can be connected quite definitely with the service of John of Gaunt. On 22 September, just when Wickham's disgrace was being prepared, he was summoned from Oxford to appear before the council. This was merely the prelude to his despatch to stir public opinion against his patron's victim. For the autumn months saw him stumping the pulpits of London, 'running about from church to church', in furtherance of Gaunt's new anti-clerical manœuvre. A disagreeable impression must be created by his willingness to act the part of Lancaster's clerical hireling. The most favourable interpretation possible for this episode is that he was in politics little better than a child. After all, Wickham, if he was nothing else (and he was indeed much else), was at least a generous patron of poor scholars. Within hardly more than a stone's-throw of Wycliffe's room at Oxford, the bishop's New College, founded on more princely lines than any other then in existence, was in process of building just at that very time. As a result of their founder's temporary financial ruin, the students there were obliged to go home. The excuse generally made for Wycliffe that 'politics make strange bedfellows' is the best evidence of how poorly endowed he has left his apologists. To make a martyr of one able if ambitious prelate cannot have much advanced the cause of reform, though it may have increased his value for Lancaster.

One of Wycliffe's chief counts against those who, like Wickham, owed their advancement in the church to their sovereign's patronage was that it involved their continuing business in worldly occupations. Such he liked to pillory as 'Cæsarean clergy'—which is to say, churchmen who concerned themselves less with the Lord's work than Cæsar's. It is difficult to feel wholly sure that his association with Lancaster justified his bespattering the prelates with that particular brand of abuse. Nor can his attempt to incite the Londoners have been altogether successful, for when it provoked those attacked into inevitable reprisal the citizens were far from solidly of his camp.

If Wickham was unable to defend himself, he did not long stand in want of a champion. When he appeared before his accusers he was comforted by the presence by his side of William Courtenay, the young bishop of London. From that moment, though little could be done at once to save him, his cause was in sure hands. For it had attracted the services of one of the ablest and most honourable of English medieval churchmen. Justice has never been done to Courtenay's high qualities, above all to the skill and magnanimity with which he led his order through the crisis that now threatened it. Since the Reformation his has been the unpopular side, and like so many of his episcopal contemporaries he has suffered unduly from protestant ignorance and misrepresentation. As at all times, though perhaps less so than at most, the English bench of bishops in the fourteenth century contained a proportion of dead wood. By citing a few notorious but, in fact, untypical examples, it is easy to give the impression that they were all either ridiculous or contemptible. Yet a wearisome list of fine scholars, diligent administrators and wise pastors could be compiled to outweigh the handful of misfits by whom the class is often judged. On such a list Courtenay would deserve a topmost place; though nothing much of a scholar, he was on every other count a great churchman. No biography by one who knew him has survived and his private correspondence is lost. The finer points of his character may therefore elude our grasp; but enough can be discerned to set his pre-eminence beyond question. Since his firmness was the rock on which Wycliffe's ill-steered movement foundered, it is important that its position should be charted.

That it owed some of its strength to Courtenay's birth can scarcely be doubted. His family, descended from a certain Athon who was Sire de Courtenay in the Gâtinais soon after the year 1000, had been one of the most illustrious in northern France. At the time of the First Crusade it had given counts to Edessa, and in the thirteenth century its descendants became the Latin Emperors at Constantinople. About 1150, however, its head, Renaud de Courtenay, was driven from his wide ancestral lands by Louis VII of France and obliged to seek his fortune in the service of our Henry II. After five generations the English

Courtenays, having intermarried with the Anglo-Norman nobility, inherited the Redvers earldom of Devon together with most of its west-country estates. William Courtenay's father, Hugh, was the tenth earl; his mother, Margaret Bohun, was the grand-daughter of Edward I. Two of his brothers distinguished themselves as soldiers in the French war and were admitted to the order of the Garter. Those who believe in heredity will find it easy to account for the spirit and ability of this cadet of a warrior family in whose veins flowed the royal blood of England and Castile.

It would be idle to pretend that his being a Courtenay did not smooth his path to the episcopate. His contemporaries thought it only right that it should. Nevertheless, he owed his rapid advancement, as did other aristocratic bishops, quite as much to merit as to birth. It was not merely that he proved himself conscientious in the discharge of his various duties, that he loved order, that he had a level head. These were qualities that a good many of his colleagues shared. What particularly struck one of them about Courtenay was 'his immense humility and liberal goodness'; and his monks at Canterbury were to remember him as openhanded, 'courteous, pious and compassionate'. Even allowing a good deal for obituary exaggeration, there is enough evidence here and elsewhere to suggest that Courtenay's fearless statesmanship (of which his defence of Wickham was only the first example) did not prevent him from being easy and affable in his personal dealings.

One instance of his scrupulousness has been recorded. When John Ball, the half-crazy hedge-priest who incited the peasants to revolt in 1381, had been condemned to a traitor's death by the king's court, he was respited for two days because Courtenay 'was anxious for the safety of his soul'. The bishop was himself certainly no fanatical persecutor; in his efforts to extirpate heresy he did his best to combine mercy with firmness. It was said of him when he died that he had always used his influence amid the political strife that rent England under Richard II in favour of moderation. That he continued to enjoy that resentful king's affection after he had rated him for his

misdeeds is the best possible testimony to his good character. It may even be wrong to dismiss his reputed piety
and humility as merely conventional; at least his death
was edifying. To judge from the effigy on his tomb at
Canterbury, which may well be an attempt at portraiture,
he was a strikingly handsome man. A doctor of canon and
civil law and chancellor of Oxford University, he was a
bishop at twenty-eight. In 1376, when he espoused the
cause of Wickham, he had recently been translated from
Hereford to London and was in his thirty-fifth year. He
was in every way a worthy opponent for his cousin Lancaster. In the ensuing struggle he quite overshadowed the
conscientious but peace-loving Sudbury, who may, indeed,
have been under an obligation to the duke for his recent
advance to the primacy.

The council was against Wickham, but it remained to be
seen whether parliament and convocation would tamely
follow its lead. Within three months of the bishop's condemnation the government's need for money obliged it to
call the estates together. Meanwhile, an opportunity had
been found to strike a blow at Courtenay. In 1376 Pope
Gregory XI, having become involved in war with the state
of Florence, excommunicated its citizens everywhere and
invited the princes and cities of Christendom to lay hands
on their goods. When the English council ignored his
wishes, Gregory talked of interdicts and wrote to
Courtenay, in whose diocese many Florentines abode,
ordering him to publish the suppressed bulls. This
Courtenay did at Paul's Cross some time in January 1377.
Those Londoners who hated the Florentines as business
rivals delightedly seized the chance to plunder their ware-
houses. But the bishop's action laid him open to heavy
penalties. Summoned before the chancellor to answer for
his contempt, he was able to save himself only by a
humiliating submission. Those who gathered for parliament on 27 January were entertained by the spectacle of
Courtenay's official explaining away his master's action,
once more at Paul's Cross, while a government spokesman
denounced papal usurpations to the assembled estates.
Nevertheless, if the bishop of London had shocked some

of the city fathers by thus provoking disorder, he had won the hearts of the many to whom foreigners were always anathema. Lancaster's high-handedness towards the city was soon to enhance Courtenay's popularity there still further.

Parliament, though restive, yielded to the duke's careful management. Not so, however, did convocation when it met at St. Paul's on 3 February. Wickham, though summoned, stayed away in response to a royal command forbidding him to approach within twenty miles of the king. The question of his absence was at once raised by a group of bishops headed by Courtenay, who insisted that proceedings should be suspended until he was present. Sudbury's attempt to respect the government's express order was overborne. Wickham, whose palaces had been sequestrated, was living in retirement at Waverley abbey near Farnham, when he at length received the primate's order to attend. And 'he who aforetime was thought to excell all others in the multitude of his servants came immediately to London with a small following. There he was joyfully received by his fellow-bishops and, as became such a person, greatly honoured'. Gaunt had suffered a reverse, while Courtenay was encouraged to take the offensive.

The target, the only too obvious target, of his attack was his enemy's clerical mouthpiece. John Wycliffe's denunciation of episcopal worldlings had been staged in the heart of Courtenay's diocese and had found willing ears among Courtenay's urban flock. It was a clear case for the church's discipline. While both parliament and convocation were still in session, Wycliffe was summoned to answer for his contumacy before his ecclesiastical superiors at St. Paul's. Courtenay had at last spurred his half-hearted primate into action. The result was the most celebrated, though not the most admirable, episode in Wycliffe's life.

Those who served Gaunt could look with confidence to his protection; it was a point of honour no less than of policy with him to maintain their quarrels as his own. When, therefore, Wycliffe arrived to face his judges on the afternoon of Thursday, 19 February, his safety was assured. Not only had the duke retained the services of four doctors of divinity, chosen one from each of the mendicant orders, to conduct the defence, but he came himself, accompanied by his friends, in an attempt to overawe the court. Prominent among those with him was his latest ally, Henry Percy, the marshal of England, whose presence, bearing his silver-tipped wand of office, was a calculated insult to both civic and ecclesiastical privilege. The provocation was unwise and before the day was out Gaunt had had his first bitter experience of London's resentment. The atmosphere in the city was already highly inflammable. For some months the growth of a new spirit of turbulence there had been causing the government concern. In the summer of 1376 the investigations of the Good Parliament had led to the discovery of widespread corruption in the aldermanic body, with the result that three of its most prominent members had been removed. To such an extent had these scandals shaken public confidence that the control long exercised over the city's affairs by a group of great merchants, mostly members of the powerful victualling gilds, seemed unlikely to survive. A movement which, if it does not deserve to be termed democratic, was at least hostile to the oligarchy in power made considerable headway in the second half of 1376, until threats of the king's displeasure brought temporary peace. The rumour that Lancaster had that very morning in parliament advised the supersession of the mayor and corporation by a royal commissioner with autocratic powers was all that was required to ensure his party a hostile welcome. Civic pride was aroused and the issue had ceased to be a purely religious one.

Trouble broke out at once. What actually happened in the heat of the moment remains doubtful. It is not surprising that chroniclers who were not there tell conflicting stories. The fullest was written down at St. Albans and will be followed here. But it is necessary to remember that its author was wildly hostile to the duke. The bishops, he tells us, awaited Wycliffe's appearance in the Lady Chapel, which was beneath the great rose window at the extreme eastern end of old St. Paul's. To reach this the Lancastrians had to push their way through a throng of citizens collected in the nave. Percy's rough attempts to clear a path led to an unseemly scuffle which brought Courtenay in protest to the spot. By the time admission had been gained to the improvised court, high words had passed and tempers were already thoroughly ruffled. Little was needed to cause an explosion, and that little was at once provided by the insolent Percy. His curt invitation to Wycliffe to take a seat and make himself comfortable drew from Courtenay a reminder that the accused must stand in the presence of his judges. While the crowd of onlookers began to stir angrily, bishop and baron exchanged insults. Then Lancaster, his colour rising, came to the rescue of his hard-pressed lieutenant. Boasting of his power to humble the pride of all the bishops in the land, he warned Courtenay to put no faith in the ability of his parents to save him; their hands would be full in the attempt to save themselves. And when Courtenay made the obvious retort that his trust was in a heavenly rather than an earthly father, the exasperated duke muttered a threat to drag the bishop from his cathedral by the hair of his head. This savage aside did not fail to reach the ears of the pressing crowd of Londoners, who were provoked beyond endurance by the abuse of their pastor. So great was the resulting uproar that all thought of proceeding with the trial had to be abandoned. We are not told what was the demeanour of the silent Wycliffe, nor how the Lancastrians succeeded in fighting their way out. But no blood, it seems, was shed. From the duke's point of view the outcome was not wholly satisfactory. While he could congratulate himself on having foiled the bishops' immediate purpose, he must soon have had cause to ask himself whether victory had not been gained at too great a cost. His aim, after all, in calling Wycliffe to London had been to whip up support for his campaign against Wickham; but the only solid result was to increase his own unpopularity in the capital. If he remained in any doubt about that as he took his way home from the fracas in St. Paul's, he was given conclusive proof of it on the morrow.

As the Good Parliament had made all too clear, he could not rely for support in his conduct of affairs on more than a section of the baronage. It was typical of the disharmony which made government by council so feeble a substitute for personal monarchy that the next outbreak by the Londoners against him was fomented by lesser members of his own class. On 20 February a meeting of citizens took place to consider what should be done to safeguard their threatened liberties. Their deliberations were cut short by the appearance of two lords, Walter Fitzwalter and Guy Brian, with the news that Percy was holding a man captive in his town house beside Aldersgate. This evidence that the marshal had exercised his disputed right of arrest within the boundaries of the city produced a riot. An armed mob rushed off to storm and ransack Percy's inn, and removed his prisoner to the civic gaol at Newgate. Luckily for himself, Percy was not at home. The rioters' next objective was Lancaster's own great palace of the Savoy. As they streamed west along Fleet Street, their two enemies were just sitting down to dinner as the guests of Sir John Ipres, one of Gaunt's most trusted servants, in another quarter of the town. The oysters had hardly been placed on the table when a messenger rushed in to warn the diners of their peril. It is reported that the duke started up in such haste that he barked both his shins against the form. Refusing the wine that was offered them, he and his ally hurried down to the Thames and fled by boat to take shelter with the Black Prince's widow at Kennington in Surrey.

Courtenay, too, had left his dinner on hearing what was afoot. Thanks to his intervention the Savoy was spared by the mob, but it was some time before the city's magistrates succeeded in restoring order. A priest who was tactless enough to voice unpopular opinions was beaten to death, the duke's arms which were displayed in Cheapside were insulted and a Lancastrian knight was roughly handled for wearing his master's hated badge. Several months passed before the citizens could be persuaded to show enough regret to induce Gaunt to agree to a reconciliation. This was brought about by the mediation of the eleven-year-old Richard II, doubtless prompted by his mother's councillors, soon after he succeeded his grandfather on the throne on 22 June 1377. But it was a hollow truce and four years later the Savoy and all its priceless treasures went up in flames at the hands of another London mob.

During the disturbances of 20 February Wycliffe's whereabouts cannot be traced, though it is not unlikely that he was already on his way back to Oxford. For the time being he was safe and no attempt was made by the prelates to resume his interrupted trial. He could still be useful to the government, and early in the new reign he was invited by the council, not necessarily on the initiative of Lancaster, to give a written opinion upon a question of law. Believing, as did most medieval statesmen, that a country's wealth depended upon its ability to conserve its supply of bullion, Richard II's advisers were alarmed at the flow of gold to the papal court, partly in taxes, partly as payment to the cardinals from the revenues of their English benefices. These latter, the commons in 1377 maintained, should be confiscated to help pay for the war. Wycliffe was therefore asked to say whether England

'might lawfully for its own defence in case of need, detain the wealth of the kingdom, so that it be not carried away in foreign parts, even though the pope himself demands it under pain of censure and by virtue of the obedience owing to him'.

This was a subject on which the scholar had, in fact, recently unburdened himself in a short pamphlet. It was customary to impose an oath upon the resident papal tax-collector to do nothing to the prejudice of the crown and realm. Wycliffe cast his views in the form of a commentary upon the oath taken in 1372 by the then collector, Arnaud Garnier, and reached the conclusion that his financial activities were so injurious to the state that he was perjured before God and man. The scholar's answer to the council's question was as uncompromising. Natural reason, the law of Christ as revealed in the Gospels and the dictates of conscience were all in favour of doing what the government wanted. As a propagandist Wycliffe was nothing if not thorough.

Meanwhile the counter-attack Wycliffe had professed to fear was being prepared against him at Avignon. His old enemies, the Benedictine monks, were naturally at the bottom of it. In view of the protection he enjoyed they had thought it unwise to oppose him openly in England; a safer way was found when it was decided to denounce him and his errors to the Roman court. Wycliffe himself afterwards laid part of the blame for his having been slandered to Gregory XI on the Benedictine bishop of Rochester, Thomas Brinton, and he may well have suspected aright. The bishop, apart from being a monk, was a close associate of Courtenay and Wickham. But there can be no doubt that the most active and influential of Wycliffe's enemies was Adam Easton, like Brinton a distinguished son of Norwich cathedral priory. Easton, who was a Hebraist with a European reputation and was soon to become a cardinal, was even then resident at Avignon. From there, on 18 November 1376, he wrote a letter to Abbot Litlington of Westminster, which identifies him unmistakably as the 'black dog' whose whelps Wycliffe held responsible for the proceedings instituted at the Curia. In it he asks the abbot to procure from his monk-students at Oxford 'a copy of the sayings of a certain Master John Wycliffe, which he disseminates, as it is said, against our order in Oxford'; he would also like to receive copies of two more of Wycliffe's works, which to judge from his description were parts of the treatises on civil and divine lordship. There is evidence that Easton must soon have obtained what he had asked for, since it was not long before he was engaged upon the composition of an elaborate reply. Still more significant, Pope Gregory had by 22 May 1377 received a list of some fifty propositions extracted from Wycliffe's recent writings on lordship, for on that day he issued a number of bulls in which eighteen were picked out for special condemnation. One bull was addressed to Edward III, one to the university of Oxford and three to Sudbury and Courtenay jointly.

Like all the missives of the venerable Roman chancery, they were couched in language that lost none of its precision by being sonorous. The bishops were watchmen sleepily nodding at their posts; the university was a slothful husbandman allowing the tares to ripen among the grain; but they were left in no doubt about what was expected of them. The errors into which the Oxford master was reported to have fallen were, it was made clear, political rather than theological, matters affecting church government, not doctrine. If he were guilty of maintaining them as true, he might be an anarchist, but he was not yet at least a heretic. It had first to be seen whether, in fact, he had really taught them. Sudbury and Courtenay were therefore to begin by informing themselves privately whether the report was true. Should the result of enquiry be unfavourable they were 'to cause the said John to be taken and put in gaol' with the object of extorting a confession. Having sent this confession and any other statement offered to Avignon under seal, they were to keep their prisoner in chains until they received fresh instructions. If he obtained secret intelligence of his impending arrest and effected an escape, they were to cite him publicly to appear before the papal court within three months. The two prelates were also urged to use their best endeavours to convince the king, the princes of the blood, the nobility and council that the condemned teaching was not merely erroneous, but subversive of all government. On the university was laid the duty of handing over Wycliffe and his disciples to the bishops and of seeing that his influence was stamped out; and Edward III was entreated to foster the good work. Up to this time Master John may have succeeded in persuading himself that his opinions were in agreement with the Church's teaching; henceforward, that was going to become increasingly difficult.

For some reason it was not until the end of 1377 that these bulls were received in England. The delay may have been caused by the need to get the one which had been directed to the old king readdressed to his successor; or some accident may have held them up *en route*. Nevertheless, their contents were known here before 28 November, since Bishop Brinton of Rochester boasted to the parliament that was dissolved on that day that Wycliffe's propositions had received their deserts at Avignon. According to the chroniclers the bulls were in Sudbury's hands only a few days before Christmas. They were published on 18 December. But Wycliffe was not arrested. It was thought safer merely to cite him to appear once more at St. Paul's within thirty days, while the chancellor of Oxford was ordered to consult his most learned colleagues to discover whether the conclusions had, in fact, been taught. Their findings were to be forwarded under seal to London to assist the court to make up its mind.

If it was expected that the university would take quietly to this plan to coerce its greatest ornament, its temper was misjudged. It was a corporation proud of its independence, resentful of interfering bishops. On the other hand, it had been roughly threatened by Gregory with the loss of its cherished privileges if it disobeyed his order to arrest Wycliffe and to root out his errors. It tried a middle course. Wycliffe was induced to agree to a voluntary (and, it is to be supposed, far from irksome) confinement in one of the university's halls. The chancellor, Dr. Alan Tanworth, having consulted the other resident masters of divinity, 'publicly declared in the Schools, on behalf of and with the assent of all, that the theses, though they sounded ill to the ear, were all the same true'. Their author's characteristic comment, that to suppress the truth simply 'because it sounded ill to sinners and ignoramuses would render all Holy Writ liable to condemnation', left it in doubt to which class he assigned Gregory and his cardinals.

That he had the princes of the church against him does not, in fact, seem to have greatly troubled Wycliffe. It is true that he declined to go to St. Paul's in January 1378 on the ground that the embarrassed Sudbury was plotting violence against him. But not later than the end of March he made a last appearance before the bishops in the chapel of Lambeth palace. He took with him what amounted to a royal safe-conduct, since the king's mother had sent an order by one of her knights that no judgement should be pronounced upon his case. The trial-scene has been much less vividly described for us than that of a year earlier. The St. Albans chronicler, barking from the security of his monastic kennel, was loud in his scorn for episcopal time-servers. Yet the latter can hardly be blamed for taking account of the princess's command. In any case a London mob once more broke up the proceedings at a convenient moment. The bishops were content to enjoin Wycliffe to abstain from arguing the disputed opinions both in the schools and in sermons, so that the laity should not be scandalised by dissensions within the church. It was an appeal to clerical solidarity. If there is little evidence that he took the implied prohibition seriously, at least in the treatises in which he sought to defend his position that year there is an unwonted moderation of language. He had not yet abandoned the hope of converting his accusers.

Death removed Gregory before he could do anything to spur his English lieutenants to greater vigour. Had he been succeeded in the normal way by an even moderately capable pope, things might still have gone ill for Wycliffe. Within a short time, however, not one, but two rival popes had been elected, Urban VI at Rome, Clement VII at Fondi, and the Schism deservedly called Great had begun. Wycliffe had been in his grave for more than a quarter of a century before Catholic Christendom was again united under one vicar. That his bones were not suffered to rest there in peace for long after Martin V's election in 1417 had closed the schism is a reminder to what extent his short career depended for its lack of disaster on the shameful degradation of the papal office. For the rest of his life it was unsafe to touch him. As long as two struggling claimants strove openly for the mastery of the west, neither could afford to stir up the trouble that might cost him the allegiance of the English. The latter were Urbanists, but if annoyed they might easily rat. Wycliffe had the countenance, if not the active sympathy, of several powerful members of the governing class; any attempt to bring him to book might have the effect of driving his protectors into the arms of the Clementines. Gregory's bulls were therefore forgotten; if anyone was to pluck up the tares of Wycliffe's teaching, it would have to be the English prelates acting on their own; and for some time to come these had the prudence to await a more favourable chance.

That was to arise, thanks to Wycliffe's growing intemperance, but meanwhile one danger, and that not a little one, had been avoided by Gregory's opportune removal. It was not the only piece of luck that attended the birth of the reform movement. The fact that England was virtually kingless and ruled by a loosely-knit oligarchy of barons and courtiers made it unlikely that the authority of the state would ever be brought solidly to the defence of the church. To the many who cried, 'Woe to the kingdom when the king is a child!', heresy was but one of the numerous distempers that accompanied a minority.

The year 1378 was, in fact, decisive in Wycliffe's life. He was coming to the point on the road where his actions might prove irrevocable. He was still free to retrace his steps, he could stand still or he could go on, but the choice would not much longer be his. Until the papacy had rejected his theses outright he could just conceivably have persuaded himself that they were in accord with the official teaching of the church—or at least not irreconcilable with it. But Gregory's bulls disposed of that possibility. Wycliffe had been told that what he had taught was erroneous, false, contrary to the faith and destructive of the social order. He was not the only scholar whose opinions were thus stigmatised; such wholesale condemnation was a frequent consequence of the liberty of discussion permitted in the schools. But there was only one alternative to submission and few—none up to then in England—were prepared to take it. For most men defiance of the considered opinion of the church was impossibly difficult; disagreement could not but be mistaken. To set up one's private judgement against the inherited wisdom of a divinely-ordained institution required a hardihood or a pride of which few were capable. After all, one might so easily be wrong and that would mean eternal damnation. As far as we know Wycliffe claimed no special revelation to hearten his purpose. It would have been so easy for him to recant, since submission would probably have entailed no further penalties; it might even have brought those material rewards to which he was not indifferent. For the bench of bishops to include a man or two whose youthful exuberance in the schools had been found to need correction was not unusual. Even among his own circle of disciples at Oxford Wycliffe might have found a future bishop and extirpator of heresy. That was not to be his road.

Indeed, there is no evidence that he ever considered recantation. He was, of course, in no physical danger so long as he enjoyed the patronage of the great, who had twice at least prevented his arrest. So orthodox had the English been in earlier times that the Inquisition had never been found necessary here. No machinery as yet existed by which a contumacious heretic could be put to death; thanks to the alarm Wycliffe caused, it was soon to be created. In 1378, in any case, he had not yet laid hands upon the central doctrines of the church. His courage was necessarily less physical than moral. Like a few other fourteenth-century thinkers, who shared with him the advantage of being protected by the lay power—Ockham, Marsiglio and John of Jandun are the obvious examples —he was prepared without flinching to believe authority wrong. The fact that he was neither excommunicated nor, indeed, in any serious peril during his lifetime scarcely matters. It is by this act of intellectual defiance, not by his subsequent failure to carry many others with him, that he deserves to be remembered.

It is difficult to understand why he did it and idle, perhaps, even to attempt to guess. There are too many conceivable reasons, from which only the prejudiced will find it easy to make a choice. Those who regard Wycliffe as a thinker of genius driven by an inexorable logic to attain inevitable truth are unlikely to be discouraged by the slight evidence that can be cited against them. But to a less partial eye their explanation seems to take too little account of the hesitations and inconsistencies of their hero, and, for that matter, still less of the nature of truth itself. Above all, it overlooks the obvious fact that it needed the threat of persecution to turn the politician into a heretic; the truth alone had had no such compulsive force.

If this view seems altogether too simple, the other, of a typically irascible don, consumed with intellectual pride and unwilling to admit a mistake, is not much happier. After all, Wycliffe's behaviour was most untypical and it is precisely for that reason that it needs explaining. It was also inconsistent; for it was not as if he had been a rebel all his life. It was only as an ageing scholar that he adopted a course of action that was to destroy his influence at Oxford and to slam the door to any further advancement in the church. That his frenzied attack upon institutions and doctrines he had hitherto spared was the product of disappointed ambition may be allowed as likely, though its violence still seems excessive. If any one guess is preferable it is that his head, never strong—witness the fun poked at his vanity by even his earliest critics—was turned by his success as a disputant and preacher and by the flattering attentions of the great. Finally, there remains the possibility of a physical cause, for which the medical evidence is at least suggestive. Some time in 1382, about two years before his death, Wycliffe was partially paralysed by a stroke; it was a second stroke, when he was not much more than fifty years of age, that finally killed him. The feverish but ill-directed activity of the last half-decade of his life, the confident assumption of infallibility in the face of diminishing support, the bad tactical judgement that robbed him of even minor success may all be accounted for as symptoms of that high blood-pressure from which he died. Such an explanation lacks sublimity and cannot but be distasteful to every right-minded historian of ideas, yet it may well be the simple, unattractive truth. At least, it makes more obvious sense than any other.

We can now see that the parting of the ways came in 1378, but it would be a mistake to suppose that for Wycliffe there was any question of a conscious choice. It is more likely that he was in too much of a temper to notice the direction he was taking. 'He goes farthest who knows not whither he goes.' Swept along by resentment, locked in furious conflict with a growing army of opponents, nearly single-handed himself, bad-tempered, probably ill and certainly overworked, Wycliffe was hardly in a position to see very far ahead.

What has given the contrary impression is the habit, at least as old as the fourteenth century, of treating his theological writings as if they presented a coherent system of thought, designed in advance and then carried out in instalments according to plan. It would be difficult to be more mistaken. Since these books were the children of a single mind it is natural that they should bear the marks of kinship, but to compare them with the *Summa Theologica* of St. Thomas Aquinas is to miss their whole point. They were, in the strict sense of the word, occasional, what the moment and the men demanded. They were the strokes of a desperate fighter in a war of words, not the peaceful and systematic unfolding of a considered philosophy. As they come down to us they are indeed repetitive, disorderly and incomplete. That they are also abusive and cantankerous is hardly surprising since they are the works of a bitter old man in a hurry. Most of Wycliffe's later writings are offensive, his attempts, not always over-scrupulous attempts, to destroy his opponents' case and to maintain his own.

In one other respect 1378 was a turning-point. Up to that year Wycliffe had placed his knowledge and skill at the disposal of others; he had been a hireling engaged in controversy on behalf of patrons who at least affected to tolerate his opinions. Henceforward, protected for old times' sake but no longer approved of, he fought his own battles for less material rewards.

The last known occasion on which his advocacy was of use to ministers was in a *cause célèbre* at the Gloucester Parliament of October 1378. On the previous 11 August some royal officers, attempting to recapture two prisoners who had escaped from the Tower and taken refuge in Westminster Abbey, were clumsy enough to slay one of them, and a sacristan trying to protect him, near the shrine of Edward the Confessor. This violation of the church's rights of sanctuary was too flagrant to be tolerated, and even Archbishop Sudbury did not shrink from excommunicating most of those responsible for the crime. Needless to say, he was enthusiastically seconded by Courtenay. The council retorted by ordering him 'for

to cease of his cursing' and by threatening Nicholas Litlington, the abbot of Westminster, with the loss of his
temporalities for obstructing the king's justice. The royal
case was that the dead man (the sacristan was conveniently
forgotten) was an absconding debtor guilty of treason and
had therefore no claims to sanctuary at all. So Litlington
was cited to answer for his contempt before a parliament
summoned, in order to avoid the scene of the dispute, to
the distant town of Gloucester. Here he stole a march on
his accusers by a direct appeal to the commons as they
were met for debate in the chapter-house of Gloucester
abbey. To judge from the annoyance of the councillors
he must have met with a favourable hearing. It was to
counteract its effect that Wycliffe was sent for. He and a
nameless doctor of laws were by the abetment of two of
the King's household knights, Sir Simon Burley and Sir
Thomas Percy, put up to answer Litlington to the commons. The task was undertaken with his usual thorough-
ness. It is nearly certain that he was also one of the
doctors who were employed by the council to demolish the
arguments of the prelates before the king in full parliament. After that the parties seem to have grown tired of
their dispute and to have shelved it. Wycliffe, with more
persistence, worked up the views he had expounded and
later published them as part of a larger book. And thus,
with a characteristic failure to mould events decisively, he
vanished for ever from the political scene.

It has been said of him by one of his most sympathetic
modern interpreters that he accomplished little in politics
'except perhaps his own disillusionment'. Even the proviso
is doubtful. It is not easy to avoid the impression that he
remained convinced to the very end of his ability to guide
men by the light of reason, little though his experience
justified this belief. It is a delusion common among
academic orators. That Wycliffe was a more persuasive
advocate than the tedious prolixity of his writing might
lead one to expect is vouched for by the frequency with
which he was employed. Had parliaments or councils to
be won over by a learned and well-argued discourse, had
a crowd to be roused by a sermon, he was evidently a use-

Chapter Four

Wycliffe the Heretic and his First Disciples

THE outbreak of the schism freed Wycliffe from the danger of further persecution by the Roman Curia, but that does not mean that he welcomed it. On the contrary, it horrified him. Like all his countrymen who were obsessed by the fear of a French pope, he was at first a wholehearted supporter of the Italian Urban VI. It was not until later that the evils attendant on this prolonged division of Catholic Christendom began to shake his faith in the papacy as an institution and caused him to regard the rival popes as the two halves of antichrist. In 1378 'our Urban' appeared to him to be the saviour of a church undermined by the wickedness of that 'horrible fiend' Gregory XI. Indeed, he went so far as to address a letter to the new pope, excusing himself from answering in person Gregory's still valid citation to Rome and protesting his humble willingness to be corrected, 'if need be by death', should he have taught or uttered anything erroneous. But lest this dovelike meekness be read as betokening a change of heart, it is as well to note that in the next breath he spoke venomously of the likelihood of Urban's being deceived by malicious councillors in his own house. The venom was presumably not factitious; one is less certain about the humility. Nevertheless, it is clear that for the time, at least, Wycliffe desired no breach with Rome. Why that desire failed before long is not so obvious. That it did can be easily traced in his works.

The five years and more that lie between the abortive Lambeth 'trial' and the onslaught of paralysis in 1382 were some of the most prolific in his life. A series of books, remarkable in bulk even when full allowance is made for his habitual borrowings from other writers and the possibility that some sections may have been rehashed from earlier lectures, poured from his pen. Otherwise, as far as the external events of his life are concerned, the period is all but blank. There is evidence that he kept his rooms in Queen's until at least the summer of 1381, and that when a year later the university was purged of its leading heretics he had already withdrawn to his rectory at Lutterworth. Almost the only fixed point on which reliance can be placed is 10 May 1381, when he published his *Confession*, a general defence of his extremer views. There are reasonable grounds for thinking that up to and beyond that time he was usually resident at Oxford, but the precise moment of his final retirement from his academic arena must continue in doubt. Even the order and date of publication of his works are largely conjectural.

The group that has been assigned to 1378 reveals how sore his treatment at the hands of pope and hierarchy had left him. It also shows his impatience with those schoolmen who sided with his persecutors. He was beginning to be freely criticised for his extreme reliance upon scriptural authority in preference to the accumulated wisdom of the church. There was substance in the charge. Thus the *Protestation* in which at Lambeth he had maintained his suspect opinions was little more than a string of biblical texts. Given the nature of Holy Writ and the ingenuity of interpretation that had already for centuries been expended on it, it was inevitable that the meanings he attached to the passages he cited should be called in question. The attitude of certain unnamed 'modern theologians' particularly annoyed him by its scepticism. The result was his large treatise *On the Truth of Holy Scripture*, the eleventh of whose thirty-two chapters is dated 25 March 1378, an incoherent and hastily assembled defence of the literal inspiration of the Bible against those clever ones who doubted it. He accepted scripture as God's Law and founded his conclusions upon it, only to have them condemned. The real heretics were rather such as professed to find inconsistencies and obscurities in its wording and held it to be in need of official interpretation. Wycliffe does not seem to have thought any form of interpretation necessary. The Bible could safely be placed in the hands of even the most ignorant: 'all Christians, and lay lords in particular, ought to know holy writ and to defend it'; and again elsewhere, 'no man is so rude a scholar but that he may learn the words of the Gospel according to his simplicity'. If these precepts were to be taken seriously, the Bible had to be made more generally available than it was in the Latin Vulgate text. Its translation into vernacular English was bound to become before long the concern of anyone who felt as strongly about it as that.

In emphasising the supreme importance of the literal sense for the right understanding of the Bible, Wycliffe was no innovator. The Franciscan Nicholas de Lyra (died 1340), a Hebrew scholar of distinction whom Wycliffe himself praises highly as a biblical commentator, Marsilio of Padua (1270–1342) and many lesser fourteenth-century schoolmen had already urged the same view; and in so far as there was what might be called an English tradition of interpretation, it had a like bias. Indeed, as readers of his works know to their cost, Wycliffe was not wholehearted in his practice of the rule he preached so fervently. But the painfully literal translation of the Scriptures which he inspired and may have supervised bears witness to his faith.

To exalt the authority of the Bible was only one-half of Wycliffe's purpose; the other was to depress that of the church which was misguided enough to reject his teaching. In a miscellany entitled *On the Church*, which also belongs to the year 1378, he set about this part of his task with a will. By 'the church', he tells us, men popularly mean 'prelates and priests, monks and canons and friars', in short, the clergy; this is a vulgar error. So too is that which describes the church as the community of all faithful believers, clerk and lay, alive and dead, since this overlooks the fact that anyone may believe and yet for want of God's grace be damned. No, the church is restricted to those predestined for salvation, the elect. The rest of mankind, lacking grace, is 'foreknown' to damnation. Wycliffe, thus, was an uncompromising predestinarian. He derived his grisly creed from Thomas Bradwardine (died 1349) and—with important differences—from their common master, Augustine. No man, he believed, knew whether he were numbered among the elect; not even the pope himself 'whether he be of the church or whether he be a limb of the fiend'. Christ was the redeemer of only a fraction of mankind; the rest, the foreknown, were the subjects of antichrist, though by a contradiction Wycliffe was unable to resolve they might derive some advantage from the sacraments.

The practical bearing of this dualistic theory is perhaps not very clear. But since one could never be sure whether the pope was or was not damned for all eternity, it was obviously unsafe to put much confidence in him. Again, it was useless to pray for the dead—or, if it came to that, for the living—if the fate of each man had already been determined by God when the world was born. Like so much of Wycliffe's theology, his predestinarianism had a destructive, almost an anarchistic, tendency. If grace were subject to the arbitrary will of the Creator alone, most human efforts became pointless. Was there any reason for believing that Wycliffe himself was one of the elect? And if not, what followed?

In *On the Office of King* Wycliffe turns back once more to consider the problem of the relative importance of church and state. In a series of curious arguments the primacy is accorded to the temporal power. If the pope is the vicar of Christ, the king is the vicar of God the Father; the one represents the humanity, the other the divinity, of Jesus. It therefore follows that the temporal ruler, however unjust, is above all human laws and must be held in honour just as Cæsar and Pilate were by Christ. It also follows that it is his duty, if need be, to reform the church. Wycliffe then gives examples of the kind of abuse he would like to see corrected: the pursuit of worldly offices and honours, the possession of temporal lordship, the sin of simony. The clergy, he asserted, must be made to live, like the Levites of old, on their tithes and whatever the faithful were moved to offer them by way of alms, surrendering all else to the laity as having been acquired without scriptural authority. The king should compel bishops to oversee more thoroughly than hitherto the morals and attainments of those holding cures in their dioceses, tithes should be withheld from all non-residents and only those properly qualified as theologians should be nominated to vacant benefices. Tacked on to this un- usually concise book is a series of postscripts which seek to forestall the obvious objections. It is interesting to find that as late as 1379, when he was writing this, Wycliffe was still hopeful of the government's intervention on his behalf in his quarrel with his ecclesiastical superiors. At least, his treatise was a determined bid for the laity's sup- port.

Enough has been said to give the reader some idea of the character of Wycliffe's writings, though nothing short of the originals themselves could convey an adequate im- pression of the tireless vitality with which each distinction is elaborated, each argument sustained and embellished, each objector met. The author's belief in his intellectual instrument is absolute. At the same time he makes no attempt to render his matter attractive to minds more frivolous than his own. Reading him may be magnificent, but it is not fun; the rare elephantine caper he permits himself merely calls attention to the unrelieved sobriety of his performance judged as a whole. The achievement is in some ways made all the more impressive by its grace- lessness and lack of polish. Those who believe that 'in the middle ages the members of the ruling class were in general men of arrested intellectual development' are at least right to credit their university-trained servants with precise minds sharpened by long exercise on the subtleties of the schools. And among these latter Wycliffe was justifiably regarded as a master.

By 1379 he was ready to turn his attention to the central mystery of the Eucharist. He had demonstrated at great length early in that year that historically and doctrinally the powers claimed by the papacy lacked the slightest foundation. Having thus made away first with the church and then with its earthly head, he was still left to dispose of the powers that might be thought to reside in the priestly office itself. If their ability to perform the miracle of the Mass were allowed to confer a special character upon members of the priesthood, their superiority to the laity might have to be admitted. Wycliffe's realist metaphysic had long made it difficult for him to accept the divorce between appearance and reality which the Catholic doctrine of transubstantiation demanded. He could not happily believe that the consecrated elements, while remaining bread and wine to the senses, had yet been changed into the substance of the Body and Blood of Christ. But although it offended his philosophical assumptions, he was for years willing enough to accept it as an unexplained mystery. Indeed, as late as in his treatise *On Civil Dominion,* he goes out of his way to subscribe gratuitously to the orthodox view. Although others were unkind enough to point out the inconsistencies which his realism gave rise to, he himself was content to avert his eyes until his quarrel with the church excited his iconoclasm. The result was a course of lectures, afterwards embodied in a book, *On the Eucharist.*

It is easier to understand Wycliffe's reasons for denying the Real Presence as it was then officially defined than to be sure by what theory he wished to replace it. His objections to transubstantiation were that it exaggerated unduly and even dangerously the importance of the priestly office, that it exposed Christ's body to the chances of daily accident and indignity, and that its grossness encouraged men to become idolatrous. He therefore set himself to demonstrate that it was contrary to the obvious sense of the Gospels, historically of quite recent origin and philosophically absurd. In the alternative explanation which he propounded he approached what is known as 'receptionism', the view which makes the nature of the thing received, namely the consecrated elements, depend upon the state of the communicant receiving it. If Christ's body was present, it was present not essentially nor even corporeally but only figuratively. It is not surprising that Wycliffe's opponents complained that he had failed to make himself intelligible. The truth seems to have been that he was not sure himself what to think. He found it less difficult to see where others had gone wrong than to decide what was right. And therefore during the short remainder of his life he struggled vainly to work out a definition that would satisfy him, as he moved steadily farther and farther away from the eucharistic doctrine of the Church.

It is permissible for the historian to think that Wycliffe's arguments from history are the most interesting if not the most original part of his book. From whom he derived his use of the historical method is uncertain, but this was by no means the first time he had employed it himself. It had already paid good dividends in his attack upon the papacy. As his *On the Power of the Pope* shows, he was acutely aware of the contrast between the institutions and doctrines of the primitive church and those that prevailed in his own day. Now he was delighted to be able to demonstrate that transubstantiation had not become Catholic dogma until the reign of Pope Innocent III (1198–1216). The Bible, the Fathers, the liturgy and the church's own teaching until the twelfth century were not unmistakably in its favour. In rejecting modern developments and urging a return to the faith and practice of the early Christians, Wycliffe belongs truly to the company of the sixteenth-century reformers. Any departure from ancient custom could for him only be due to the machinations of antichrist.

It is sometimes implied that what made Wycliffe a rebel against the established order was his moral indignation at the abuses from which the church along with society as a whole was suffering. For this there is strikingly little justification in his works; and it would only square with the known facts of his life on the assumption that he underwent some sort of conversion near its end, an incident otherwise totally unrecorded and in any event somewhat improbable. This view is so contrary to the general impression conveyed by Wycliffe's other biographers that it may seem to require some slight elaboration. It would admittedly be possible to assemble a long list of passages in which Wycliffe denounces in suitably indignant terms the vices of popes, bishops, monks and, after they had deserted his cause, friars. His opinions on pluralism, non-residence and the other faults of the lesser clergy were just as unfavourable. But two things need to be remembered before any sweeping conclusions are drawn from such hostile criticism. Firstly, they were the veriest commonplaces of fourteenth-century controversy, when the rivalries of the various orders within the church encouraged such extravagance, were the subject-matter of hundreds of surviving sermons and were as much the stock-in-trade of poets like John Langland as of the preachers and scholars of Wycliffe's own class. If the utterance of such conventional coin signified that their authors were full of zeal for reform, then one is forced to conclude that the reformers of fourteenth-century England were even more numerous than those in need of reformation. To the habit of taking such diatribes seriously can be traced most of the distortion common to all modern pictures of the later medieval church. In the second place it cannot be reasonably maintained as far as Wycliffe was concerned that denunciation of the failings of the clergy was the main purpose of his writing; it is at best subordinate, thrown in to make up full measure. This may not have been true, it is only fair to add, in the case of some of his less educated followers, but these were generally incapable of appreciating the finer points of his thought. If the Wycliffite movement ever became fiercely critical of moral abuses in the church, it was largely because it had lost touch with the intellectual interests of its founder; and as it became more and more lay in composition, that became increasingly true.

It is only when, as a result of his eucharistic heresies, Wycliffe was deserted by most of his allies and sympathisers that it is possible to distinguish from them that group of men to whom it is fitting to apply the name disciples. Until 1378 or 1379, indeed, it is doubtful whether many outside Oxford were able to recognise any important differences between his teaching and that of the numerous spokesmen of the anti-clerical interest. Nor is there any evidence that the attempt of the bishops to silence him affected his popularity much one way or the other, though its failure may well have confirmed the impression that his was the winning cause. The academic world, on the other hand, had long known of his association with what may be called the 'left wing' among the mendicants, and even some who were ready to go far with him in politics were already uneasily aware of the heretical implications of his thought. Those whom he had attacked, especially the monk scholars, had for some time been actively engaged in replying to his arguments. His denial of transubstantiation gave them the chance they needed to carry the war decisively into his own country. The first result, it seems, was his loss of most, if not all, of the support that he had received from the friars. One amusing instance of this has recently come to light.[1] In the notebook of an industrious young Austin friar of the Cambridge house, by name Adam Stockton, will be found a copy of one of Wycliffe's most violent anti-papal broadsides, written in 1379. Against it Stockton noted that it was by the 'venerable doctor, Master John Wycliffe'; soon afterwards, in 1380 or 1381, he crossed out the first two words quoted and substituted, without comment, 'execrable seducer'; even this callow admirer at length realised his danger. The fact that about this time a new note of biting criticism is heard in Wycliffe's references to the friars suggested that the warier fellow-travellers among them had already taken themselves off.

The alarm was sounded at Oxford round about midwinter 1380–1. The chancellor, William Barton, a fellow of Merton and a doctor of divinity who had opposed Wycliffe's doctrines in the schools, decided that the time had come when official action could safely be taken. He therefore appointed a commission, consisting of twelve doctors, six of them friars, four seculars and two monks, to report on their colleague's eucharistic teaching. It is difficult to accept the assertion that this body was packed.

---

[1] It was discovered by the Rev. A. Gwynn, S.J. See his *English Austin Friars in the Time of Wyclif*, pp. 236–9 and 253–4.

If it were, then it was done most inefficiently. According to Wycliffe himself it reported against him only by the barest possible majority. One of its members, Richard Rigg, was soon to expose himself to reprisals by his patronage of Wycliffe's rasher followers. And in any case an acquittal would have been straight contrary to the evidence. The fact that five men were prepared to vote for it can only mean that they had not been chosen by Barton to condemn Wycliffe out of hand. The division of opinion probably represents fairly faithfully the state of mind of the university, or at least of its seniors, in this transitional period. The majority of seven found the charge of maintaining erroneous doctrines proved, and the chancellor threatened those holding, teaching or defending them with imprisonment, suspension from all university functions and excommunication. The last penalty was also reserved for those who failed to flee such heretical teachers as they would a venomous snake.

Wycliffe was seated disputing in the 'school' of the Austin friars, near where Wadham College now is, when the verdict and sentence were read to him publicly. An authority by no means friendly to him gives what is still probably a truthful description of the effect: 'on hearing this condemnation he was confused; but yet he said that neither the chancellor nor any of his accomplices could in the least weaken his opinion.' After thinking the matter over he decided to appeal, not to any ecclesiastical court, to which even in the eyes of English law the appellate jurisdiction in matters of faith belonged, but to the king. We are left to gather that his appeal was in strict form ignored, but John of Gaunt is said to have hurried down to Oxford in an attempt to induce his old henchman to obey the chancellor's prohibition. It would be rash to put over-much belief in the duke's visit, but the attitude of alarmed disapproval with which he is credited does almost certainly reflect the feelings of the nobility at the scholar's growing intransigence.

Wycliffe ignored his patron's wishes. His publication of his *Confession* on 10 May 1381, in which he defended the condemned opinions, meant the loss of the only supporters who had the power, and might have had the will, to carry out the more modest of his proposals: some disendowment, accompanied by greater control by the state in ecclesiastical affairs. To suppose that there could have been any sort of reformation in England, let alone a breach with Rome or a change of doctrine, without the active help of at least a powerful minority of the nobility and gentry betokens a wilful blindness to the political realities of fourteenth-century English society almost as great as Wycliffe's own. Even in countries like Germany, where the central authority was weak, a popular religious movement needed princely backing. In a strong centralised state, such as by comparison England was even in a time of royal minority, the support of the court and the governing classes was a first condition of success. The reformation of the sixteenth century could, indeed, never have happened without it. Wycliffe, by his headlong advocacy of doctrinal changes, for which the upper classes were then even less prepared than were their descendants under the Tudors, did his utmost to discredit not only the moderate parts of his programme, but reform of any sort for many years to come.

By publishing the *Confession* Wycliffe was intent on little more than saving his face. He might bluster defiantly at those who had condemned his teaching, but his actions belied his words. That spring was his last in Oxford; soon afterwards he seems to have withdrawn finally from the university in which his whole working life had been spent to the isolation and obscurity of Lutterworth. When the day came for his disciples to face tribulation it was under other leadership than his.

If anything was necessary to complete the disillusion of his former lay sympathisers it was the Peasants' Revolt of June 1381. There is little reason to think that his teaching was responsible for the rising, still less that the rebels had his active encouragement or support. His enemies could not be prevented, however, from throwing the blame on him and, thanks to his notorious claim that the just alone had a right to their possessions, with something like a show of plausibility. A number of lesser clergy, of whom

John Ball was the most conspicuous, had without the least doubt contributed to the disturbances by their inflammatory preaching; and some had been prominent in the camps of the rebels. To make out that they were the followers of Wycliffe and thereby to discredit him was a chance too good to be missed. It was rumoured, on the strength of a confession that does not survive, that Ball had admitted to having been for two years the Oxford heretic's pupil. But Ball had, in fact, been a troublesome demagogue long before Wycliffe turned his mind to politics; and the minute researches of M. André Réville and other modern scholars have completely failed to establish any connection between the two men or their associates. Nevertheless, Wycliffe had uttered views which, however theoretical he intended their application to be, might easily be mistaken by the ignorant for an attack on the sanctity of private property; and it is hardly surprising that the landed classes, their confidence in their security roughly demolished by the sudden impact of the revolt, should have found it difficult to acquit him of incitement. If heresy by itself had not been enough to frighten them, heresy and sedition combined were. Most of them, though they did not at once lose their dislike of episcopal authoritarianism, were soon prepared to acquiesce in the policy of repression demanded by Courtenay.

The popular name by which Wycliffe's followers about this time came to be known was that of 'Lollards'. The word, which signifies mumblers, was not new, having been opprobriously applied to heretics before. For that reason it was never strictly confined to those holding a particular set of doctrines, and many who were called Lollards were not Wycliffites. What is more, like 'Fascist beast' or 'Red' today, the name before long grew to be a loose term of disparagement for those whose views the speaker or writer hated and wished to injure in the eyes of others. Its use does not, therefore, make the task of identifying the genuine disciples of Wycliffe any simpler. But the truth is that before they had been provided by him with such unmistakable trappings as the eucharistic heresies of his last years, there was nothing to differentiate them clearly from the mass of reformers then abounding. Nor was there, indeed, any reason for them to wish to differentiate themselves. What the poet Gower in 1390 could call 'this new sect of Lollardy' was in process of slow formation after 1379.

Precisely when it came into being and by whose agency are matters always likely to remain doubtful. Until persecution brought some Lollards an unsought notoriety, their very existence left few traces in contemporary record. Chroniclers, writing well after the event, were not merely vague but contradicted one another about the date when the movement began, one group favouring 1377, the other 1382. There is scarcely any doubt which comes nearer the truth. Since those who prefer the earlier year seriously antedate Wycliffe's denial of transubstantiation, they are not to be treated as reliable. In any case it is hard to believe that by 1377 Wycliffe was ready to take the decisive step of sending his apostles, clad in russet gowns and barefoot like pilgrims, on missionary journeys round England. The view that not only did he not do it then but never did it is, to say the least, a tenable one; since by 1382, when there is indisputable evidence of unlicensed Lollard preaching, he was no longer at Oxford, and there is nothing then or later to connect his refuge at Lutterworth with the movement. The dispatch of missionaries on tour may well have been the work of the younger hotheads whom he had left behind in the university and who would shortly be disciplined for their pains. Against this must be set the fervent belief of modern writers that Wycliffe's books from 1377 onwards contain frequent references under various names to his 'Poor Priests'. But an examination of the cited passages lends no support whatever to this hypothesis; the possessive pronoun and the capital letters had no contemporary warrant and to call the Wycliffites 'Poor Priests' is to be guilty of a nineteenth-century anachronism.

Who, then, were the earliest Lollards? Apart from those who shared the master's retirement at Lutterworth and who like him were for the moment quiet, the answer would seem to be the group of secular clerks in residence at Oxford who first got into trouble with the authorities in the spring of 1382. Their leader, Nicholas Hereford, is something more than a name to us. At that time he was a doctor of divinity and had probably been engaged since about 1380 in translating the Latin version of the Bible into English. Hereford may, like Wycliffe, have been cheated of hoped-for promotion in the church by the workings of Gregory XI's patronage system. From 1369 to 1375 he had held a fellowship at Queen's College and may be presumed to have owed his conversion to Lollardy to an acquaintance with Wycliffe dating from that time. According to the St. Albans chronicler, he was 'the most violent' of his master's followers; his later activities prove him to have been impulsive and unstable as well, of a type, in fact, common in the early annals of most religious movements. With him were associated two other west-countrymen: John Aston, a B.D. belonging to the diocese of Worcester, and Laurence Steven (*alias* Bedman) from Cornwall, who had been a fellow and for a short time (1377–80) rector of Exeter College. Steven's enthusiasm was of short duration and his unorthodoxy doubtful, but Aston was a tougher sectary. Not only is he described as having presumed to add to Wycliffe's 'errors' others of his own, but we are told how he made converts of simple men by talking to them at table and took to the roads on foot 'like a bee'. Although something of a scholar, he was perhaps better suited than most of the academic Lollards for the more demagogic phase of their work which was the outcome of their expulsion from Oxford. Other early members of the group like Robert Alington, probably also a Queen's man, and John Ashwardby, the vicar of St. Mary's (from the pulpit of which Wesley and Newman were to preach to two other Oxford movements), have left little trace of their work.

The most recent, and for a time almost the keenest, convert was Philip Repton, a young Austin canon of the abbey of St. Mary-in-the-Fields by Leicester, who proceeded to the degree of D.D. towards the end of summer term 1382. It was not many months since he had proclaimed his attachment to Wycliffe's sacramental teaching in a sermon at Brackley in Northamptonshire, of which the Leicester canons were rectors. The existence of a number of Lollards, even at this early date, among the inhabitants of Leicester itself may be the product of his evangelism. The alternative, and more usual, explanation that it was due to Wycliffe's influence from Lutterworth, not fifteen miles away, has less plausibility. The local historian Knighton, so full in other respects, is vague on this one point; but while he may have had reasons for not mentioning Repton, the man who before so very long became his abbot at St. Mary's and later his diocesan bishop, he would have been the first to make the arch-heretic personally responsible had there been any excuse for doing so. There is, moreover, no evidence that Lutter-worth was ever a centre of heresy in spite of Wycliffe's presence there; and when episcopal correction was in 1382 administered to those Lollards who had been active in Leicester and its neighbourhood, the founder of the sect and his household excited no remark. The discoverable links between him and the more popular side of the move-ment he inspired are extraordinarily flimsy.

But whether or no Repton planted the seed at Leices-ter, it soon sprang up most vigorously. This was thanks to the zeal of two very different men, William Smith and William Swinderby. Smith would be interesting, if for no other reason, because he was the first layman of many associated with the Lollard movment. Even the trade from which he derived his name takes us down into that class of manual craftsmen where most of the later mem-bers of the sect were to be found. According to the gossip of an unfriendly eyewitness, Smith was deformed and ugly. His inability to persuade a young woman to become his wife led him to renounce the flesh and the wearing of shoes, to become a vegetarian and a teetotaller and, finally, to teach himself to read and write. Joined by a chaplain called Waytestathe, he established himself in a deserted chapel dedicated to the Baptist hard by the leper hospital without the walls of Leicester, where he began to hold conventicles for the disaffected townsfolk and to keep a Lollard school. The venture prospered, with the result that he was soon joined in his retreat by Swinderby, popularly known as 'William the Hermit', an eccentric but talented member of that clerical underworld to which Lollard revivalism was beginning to appeal.

Swinderby had denounced and renounced a good many things in his day. The first object of his scorn had been the pride and wantonness of women, until the good wives of Leicester and other ladies less good threatened to stone him from the town. Thereupon he turned his eloquence against wealth and merchandising; as a result of which so many despaired of salvation that he grew quite unpopular again. Tiring of this, he next became a hermit in the neighbouring woods, where he seems to have enjoyed the favour of the landlord, John of Gaunt. But this did not amuse him for long and he was soon back in Leicester, using a cell in St. Mary's Abbey as his headquarters for a series of preaching tours among the surrounding villages. It was then that he was attracted to throw in his lot with the inmates of St. John's chapel. Hitherto his antics had been puritan rather than Lollard, as if he were more akin to John Ball than to the heretic schoolmen of Oxford; and even his later utterances, if it is safe to judge from the sketchy reports that have come down to us, contained only a very watery and simplified version of Wycliffe's novel doctrines. Swinderby was indeed, like Smith, a portent; he was the first of a number of half-educated and usually unbeneficed mass-priests who were the main channel by which Lollardy was to be transmitted to future generations. For them the right of the laity to withhold tithes from incompetent parsons and even to dispense with a ministry altogether were questions of greater moment than realist metaphysics or the nature of lordship. Even in the founder's own lifetime the character of the movement was becoming less academic, more popular.

Apart from Oxford and Leicester with their very different spirits, there were no other known centres of Lollardy before 1382. But from these two, daughter-cells may already have been planted about the countryside. Swinderby, for example, seems to have been heard as a preacher, not only in Leicester, but at Melton Mowbray,

Hallaton, Market Harborough and Loughborough; and it is to be presumed that he gained a number of converts. Similarly, Hereford and his friends were invited down to Odiham in north-east Hampshire by a vicar who evidently had a taste for their sermons and may therefore have been educated at Oxford himself. At first the bishops thought it best to wink at these goings-on and did nothing to molest the itinerants, but this period of immunity was brought to an abrupt end by the elevation of William Courtenay to the primacy in the spring of 1382.[1] Wycliffe's old enemy at once set about the eradication of Lollardy from his province, spurred on to the work, it is said, by a request for action from the parliament called in November 1381 to endorse the king's suppression of the Peasants' Revolt. The outcome was the meeting of the so-called 'Earthquake Council' of 17 May 1382 at the house of the Black Friars in London.

To counter the archbishop's attack Wycliffe chose this moment to make his last known appeal for lay support in a memorial of seven points (or, as he called them, 'imprecations'), which he addressed to the parliament of 7–22 May. Eschewing those doctrinal heresies for which he could expect little sympathy, he concentrated on matters likely to appeal to a patriotic audience, the exclusion of the clergy from the government's service, the prohibition of all payments to Rome, the confiscation of the benefices of absentee cardinals and the use of the church's endowments to save the people from direct taxation. In vain; the records of parliament show no sign that these proposals ever received consideration. They certainly failed to deflect Courtenay from his purpose.

The archbishop rightly concentrated his attention upon Oxford, leaving his suffragans to deal in their own dioceses with any heretical invaders. The university seems to have been a good deal disturbed that spring by one of its recurrent outbreaks of ill-feeling between seculars and mendicants. It was only natural that Hereford and his

---

[1] Although elected by the monks of Canterbury on 30 July 1381, he did not receive the *pallium* from Urban VI until the following 6 May.

fellow-Lollards should have been prominent among the former. On 18 February the heads of the four mendicant houses addressed a letter of appeal against their attacks to the duke of Lancaster. A few days later, Hereford, preaching in Latin before an academic audience in St. Mary's, argued that any clerk who was a member of a religious order committed apostasy by taking a degree. This was a scholastic way of saying that monks and friars had no business at the university and seems to have gone down well with Hereford's fellow-seculars. Not only did the two proctors join in the applause, but Robert Rigg, the chancellor, when applied to, declined to interfere.

For Courtenay the first essential was a condemnation of Wycliffe's opinions in as formal and authoritative a fashion as possible. This required a good deal of management. Disaffection had spread so far, especially among the secular masters, whose dislike of episcopal interference in the affairs of the university always made them difficult to handle, that the archbishop had to risk the possible retort that his council was unrepresentative. It may have been so, but its composition was none the less distinguished. At the first session there were present, besides Courtenay and nine other bishops, some thirty-six graduates in theology or law as well as many lesser clergy. But a critic might have noticed that of the seventeen doctors of theology assembled only one was not a friar and that he was a monk. The seculars were better represented among the lawyers, but these were less scholars than men of affairs, and one looks in vain for anyone likely to be tender to the susceptibilities of the university. To which Courtenay's answer might well have been that Oxford had become a scandal to the church and was in need of discipline.

The council's decisions were invited on twenty-four propositions drawn from Wycliffe's writings, though the author's name was nowhere officially mentioned. For one reason or another Courtenay had thought it best to leave the master undisturbed and to strike at his influence through his pupils. After four days' discussion the proceedings were brought to an end on the afternoon of

Wednesday, 21 May. Ten of the propositions were found to be heretical and the rest erroneous. The first group was well chosen to illustrate the main aspects of Wycliffe's teaching on the Eucharist, the papacy, the uselessness of confession and the indefensibility of a property-owning clergy. The end of the proceedings was marked by an earthquake which both sides hastened to claim as an expression of divine support.

The assembly also had before it evidence of the activities of unlicensed preachers, 'not only in churches and churchyards, but also in markets, fairs and other open spaces where people greatly congregate', contumaciously ignoring the bishops' attempts to suppress them. It is clear that the old and cumbersome machinery for enforcing episcopal discipline was breaking down under the test of an organised campaign of evasion. On the ground that the sowing of dissension between the estates of the realm imperilled its safety as much as the church's—an obvious reference to the Peasants' Revolt—the meeting resolved to appeal for assistance to the lay power. A petition was accordingly submitted by Courtenay to the king, who was at that time discussing business with his parliament at Westminster. The remedy proposed, having obtained the royal assent but without having been debated in the commons, was hastily tacked on to the tail-end of the statute and published through the sheriffs on 26 May. A month later, however, on 26 June, the Chancery adopted a simpler procedure, which for the next few years had to satisfy the prelates as a method of rounding up troublemakers. By this the king's officers were authorised to arrest such unlicensed preachers and their abettors as were certified to them by a bishop and to hold them, subject to an appeal to the council, until they had cleared themselves in an ecclesiastical court. When a new parliament met after Michaelmas the commons protested in vain at the way in which their approval had been taken for granted.

Meanwhile at Oxford the university was preparing to make a brave show of defiance. On Ascension Day (15 May) Nicholas Hereford was chosen by the chancellor to preach in English in the churchyard of St. Frideswide's and seized the occasion to deliver an inflammatory sermon inciting the people to rise in Wycliffe's defence. But already he was being watched and his words recorded by a certain Carmelite theologian, Dr. Peter Stokes, who throughout this critical year put himself forward, both by preaching and disputation, as the local champion of orthodoxy against Lollard attack. It was to Stokes on 28 May that Courtenay entrusted the task of publishing the decisions of the Blackfriars council to the university on the feast of Corpus Christi (5 June). It so happened that this day had been chosen for a great Lollard demonstration in which, again at the invitation of Chancellor Rigg, Philip Repton was to preach at St. Frideswide's. In the hope of preventing it, Stokes went and bearded the chancellor on 4 June. But when he produced the archbishop's commission, together with a letter in which Courtenay asked for Rigg's help, he merely met with obstruction.

We have only Stokes's account of that memorable last triumph of Oxford Lollardy, the sermon on Corpus Christi Day, and it is highly coloured. He gave the archbishop to understand that he went hourly in fear of his life, and had much to say about bands of armed men which was either intended to raise the value of his services or perhaps to excuse his failure. In fact, although the academic disputes of the period were often attended by violence, no blood seems to have been shed on this occasion. The chancellor and both proctors were there to hear Repton preach. Perhaps because Stokes was quaking in his chair at the sounds of Lollard jubilation, he does not give a very coherent précis of the sermon. Repton, it seems, maintained among other things that Wycliffe's eucharistic teaching was that of the whole church, that it was contrary to Holy Writ to mention popes and bishops in one's prayers before temporal lords and that he and his friends still enjoyed the favour of John of Gaunt. Rigg applauded with a smiling face 'and great joy came over the Lollards at such a sermon'. The week-end was spent in a round of disputations, in which by Tuesday Stokes plucked up courage to join, only to be terrified afresh by the presence of armed men in his lecture-room. The next day he was summoned by Courtenay to London to report.

The chancellor and proctors, accompanied by Thomas Brightwell, one of the masters who had come under suspicion of heresy, had preceded him there. Although not prepared to take his orders from a Carmelite, Rigg was, in fact, no Lollard. After the excitement had died down and he had had time to think, he seems to have felt that he had allowed his partisanship to carry him too far; at any rate, he had now arrived to forestall the primate's resentment. He was kept waiting for his pains until Stokes's coming had put the archbishop in possession of the facts. Then on 12 June he and Brightwell were admitted to a new session of the Blackfriars council and required to answer for their contempts. Rigg made no sort of fight, but on being shown the list of Wycliffe's heresies and errors meekly agreed to their condemnation. Flinging himself on his knees before the archbishop, he humbly begged his pardon for ignoring his commands and treating his agent with discourtesy. It was granted on the intercession of William Wickham. Brightwell hesitated rather longer, but after submitting to a diligent examination at Courtenay's hands he was convinced of his mistake. In future, if he had any doubts about the church's teaching he had the sense to keep them to himself.

Rigg had cut a poor figure, but his humiliation was not yet complete. He was next charged by the primate to do at once what he had so far evaded doing, namely, to publish the council's decrees at Oxford. His plea that it was unsafe in the then state of university opinion was angrily rejected. He was also ordered to cause Wycliffe, Hereford, Repton, Aston and Steven to be suspended from preaching and disputing until they had purged themselves of heresy, and should he find any others who shared their beliefs—and he was told to look hard—he was to compel them likewise to abjure. And lest he should show any inclination to forget Courtenay's wishes once he had escaped from his presence, he was next day hauled before the king's council and warned to do as he was told.

The publication of the Blackfriars decrees in St. Mary's

on Sunday, 15 June resulted, as the unhappy Rigg had expected, in an uproar. Nor could the chancellor himself resist one minor act of defiance, since he marked his return by suspending a certain Dr. Henry Crump, an Irish Cistercian and a member of the council that had just called him to order, for having described Hereford's party as Lollards. This got him into trouble with the government, now strongly behind the primate in his determination to impose conformity. The university's officers were instructed to reinstate Crump and forbidden to molest him, Stokes or any of their friends under pain of the royal displeasure. Wycliffe's failure to carry those in power with him was now beginning to bear fruit.

As soon as the condemned seculars learnt from Rigg that he would be obliged to proceed to their suspension, they decided to seek the aid of the duke of Lancaster. On 16 June Hereford and Repton found him living at his suburban manor of Tottenhall and even at first disposed, it is said, to give an ear to their complaints. But it only needed a deputation of more orthodox theologians to convince him that the eucharistic teaching of his Oxford visitors was detestable and for him to order them to make their peace with the archbishop. His rejection of their appeal ended, as far as we know, the duke's connection with the Lollards. They would boast no more, as Repton had so recently done, that they were sure of his protection.

The two ringleaders saw that there was nothing for it but to take his advice and submit. On 18 June, a Wednesday, they therefore made their appearance before Courtenay and a handful of assessors at Blackfriars. Cross-examined on their attitude towards the condemned opinions, they sought and obtained a day's respite in which to study them and to put down their answers in writing. Aston, who had now joined them, was rash enough to profess his willingness to be heard at once. His evasive replies made such a bad impression that he was soon warned to appear for further questioning at the larger assembly that was to try his companions on the Friday following. A little unwisely he and Hereford occupied themselves in the interval with an attempt to awaken the sympathies of the Londoners by distributing handbills in the streets of the city.

When the council met on 20 June Hereford and Repton were dealt with first. In the papers which they had drawn up they had done their best to meet criticism by agreeing that the twenty-four extracts from Wycliffe's books had all been rightly censured. But when their own comments were read out some were found of doubtful orthodoxy and others ambiguous or obscure. After a detailed examination *viva voce* they were found guilty of heresy on four counts and of error on two. Even then Courtenay still did his best to persuade them to change their minds and, undeterred by their obstinate refusal, postponed judgement for another week to give them time for reflection.

Up to this point, we are left to gather, proceedings had been carried on in orderly fashion and in Latin, but when Aston's turn came he began at once to play to the gallery by answering the questions put to him by the court not only in English, but in words of brave and insolent derision. If he hoped that the mob would once more intervene to save the accused from his ecclesiastical judges, he might have saved himself the trouble. Although his lay supporters were numerous enough to disturb the trial, they were unable to prevent his being condemned as a teacher of false doctrine. Their demonstration merely caused the archbishop to decide to hold all future sessions elsewhere, out of reach of the Londoners' turbulence. For his contumacious defiance Aston seems to have been immediately sentenced to detention in one of the primate's prisons; at any rate, no more is heard of him until he was brought before convocation at Oxford in the following November, a sadder and a meeker man.

Meanwhile Hereford and Repton, together with a minor Oxford suspect, one Thomas Hilman of Merton, were summoned to Courtenay's manor-house at Otford on 27 June to hear what he had in store for them. The archbishop, when they presented themselves on the appointed day, could not be bothered with them but cited them to appear again at Canterbury on 1 July. This time only Hilman came, stammered an apology and was reconciled.

The two ringleaders, guessing what awaited them and still in no mood to recant, failed to put in an appearance. For this they were excommunicated. In no way daunted by this, they appealed to Rome and posted notice of their action on the doors of St. Paul's and the church of St. Mary-le-Bow. Courtenay treated their schemes to evade his sentence with contempt and redoubled his efforts to bring them to heel. Their excommunication was solemnly pronounced with bell, book and candle before the people at Paul's Cross on Sunday, 13 July; and a score of mandates, not only from the indefatigable primate, but from the almost equally zealous government, showered down on the authorities of Oxford, exhorting, banning and threatening.

The accused had, however, disappeared. Hereford, with singular optimism, had hurried off to the Roman court with the intention of converting Urban VI to his master's anti-papalist views and to appeal in person against the decisions of Courtenay's Blackfriars council. Repton lay low either in Leicester or in Oxford. But he had had enough and by the autumn he was ready to admit the error of his ways. So too was Laurence Steven *alias* Bedman, who was pronounced free from heresy by Bishop Wickham and reconciled to the church at Southwark on 22 October 1382. Next day Repton appeared before the primate and a number of other bishops and doctors at Blackfriars, humbled himself, was absolved and restored to his academic status. These abjurations were permanent and, it is to be supposed, sincere.

To drive home his attack Courtenay decided to hold the next meeting of the convocation of Canterbury at Oxford and to make it an occasion for asserting his right to visit and correct the university. His clergy accordingly held their first session at St. Frideswide's on 13 November 1382. The chancellor Rigg, now anxiously compliant, preached the opening sermon. A committee of three bishops and three doctors (including Rigg) was set up to investigate the teaching of all senior members of the university, doctors, masters and bachelors alike, and to root out all error. On 24 November the contrite Repton was produced to offer the other suspects an edifying example: 'I swear by the gospels,' he declared, 'the gospels that I hold in my hand, never by any man's persuasion to defend or hold as true the aforesaid conclusions.'

The next to yield was seemingly the most obdurate. After Repton's public submission John Aston was led before the assembled prelates to be cross-examined afresh. If any among the press of graduates and undergraduates about the doors sympathised with the views that had got him into trouble, no voice dared to make itself heard. Asked to expound his teaching on the question of the Eucharist, he pleaded ignorance. Courtenay, who perhaps gathered from a more chastened bearing that he would allow himself to be persuaded, then sent him off to dine with Rigg and others. The archbishop's confidence was justified. Arguments that only a few months before had made no impression now proved unaccountably convincing. After a talk with Thomas de la Mare, the abbot of St. Albans, a formidable prelate indeed, but one more adept in worldly business than in the traffic of ideas, Aston soon professed himself won over. It only remained for the penitent heretic to read his recantation to the bishops and to apologise to Courtenay for his earlier insolence. Three days later he was absolved and reinstated.

Little more remained to be done. A feeble attempt by the defeated party to accuse Stokes and Crump of heretical teaching was scornfully rejected by the archbishop. Finally, after voting the king as small a grant of taxation as it decently could, this memorable convocation was adjourned on 26 November, having witnessed a triumph that owed everything to Courtenay's firmness and moderation. The Wycliffite heresy had been utterly routed in its principal stronghold, and the university, though never, despite appearances, wholly lost to the faith, had been decisively—and bloodlessly—recaptured. Few of its scholars, opinionated as they often were, were ready for martyrdom; hardly even the threat of persecution was needed to recall them to orthodoxy. While Aston's submission proved to be half-hearted, or at least of no great duration, that of his academic friends was in most cases lasting.

Repton's *volte-face* was typical. Forced by Courtenay's unruffled display of authority to realise clearly what was involved, he did not hesitate to devote the rest of his life and his very considerable abilities to the service of the church. His election as abbot of his house at Leicester in 1393 was the beginning of a highly successful ecclesiastical career. The abbey's patron was the duke of Lancaster, who in 1399 usurped the throne as Henry IV. Next year his *protégé* Repton became chancellor of Oxford, in 1404 the king's confessor and soon afterwards, as the result of Henry's expressed wish, bishop of Lincoln. The diocese, which stretched from the Thames to the Humber, contained its meed of Lollards and it became Bishop Philip's duty, which he performed with so much fortitude that it seemed like zeal, to persecute men for the opinions he had helped to spread. His loss to the Wycliffite cause was heavy, but many other recruits of promise deserted with him. In Oxford the fires were as good as out. Though the ashes were to flicker into flame once or twice more before becoming cold, there was no danger of a renewed conflagration.

The loss of Oxford was of vital importance to Lollardy. Wycliffe and his sympathisers had, of course, been a minority there ever since his heresies had become glaringly obvious, much as many who were doctrinally orthodox shared his desire to avoid episcopal interference. But as long as the Wycliffites retained a foothold in the university, itself the church's principal recruiting ground in England, they were in no danger of losing influence. The proceedings of 1382 virtually deprived them of the platform from which their opinions could be disseminated among the higher clergy in each new academic generation. Henceforward they were unlikely to gain neophytes from the graduates for whom all the best benefices were reserved and who alone were in a position to influence events. It also meant that, once the first generation of academic Lollards had died out, the movement would ultimately cease to be Wycliffite. If it were to keep alive at all—and that with some vicissitudes it did succeed in doing—it would gradually lose its scholarly character. Thanks to Courtenay the Lollards were fated to form a sect of semi-literates and pious laymen. The future, now that they had been expelled from their academic paradise, was bound to be with men like Smith and Swinderby rather than with the Herefords and Reptons.

Courtenay's smashing victory was achieved without any overt attempt on Wycliffe's part to defeat it. It is difficult to imagine what, indeed, the scholar could have done to hinder the primate's efforts. But at least he did not have to defend himself in person before the council at Black-friars nor in the presence of the bishops in St. Frides-wide's. He remained unmolested—as far as we know—at Lutterworth. On the other hand, the impression given by some historians that nothing whatever was done to enforce compliance upon him is very far from the truth. Though he escaped the public humiliation undergone by his chief disciples, no attempt was made to disguise the fact that it was his teaching and example that were responsible for the trouble. His name, again, heads the list of those suspected heretics whom Chancellor Rigg was ordered by Courtenay on 12 June to suspend from preach-ing and teaching until they had purged their innocence before the archbishop. It is as prominent in the king's letters to the university a month later on 13 July; these ordered the expulsion from Oxford of all who favoured the heresies and errors of Masters Wycliffe, Hereford, Repton and Aston and allowed for the seizure of all books and treatises edited or compiled by the two first-named. It was only when on 30 July Courtenay ordered that the excommunication of Hereford and Repton should be read in every church in his province that references to Wycliffe disappear. It is not surprising that some otherwise well-informed contemporaries believed that the master had presented himself and made his submission. They may only be wrong in supposing that this occurred publicly at Oxford. That he gave Courtenay or the latter's agents a private undertaking in return for immunity from persecu-tion is not unlikely. At any rate, in a book which he wrote shortly afterwards he mentions that he had pledged himself not to use certain words about the sacrament 'outside the schools'. Since he had already been suspended from teaching within the university, this amounted to an absolute silence. But whatever this may have done to his tongue it is fair to add that it had precious little effect on his pen. Presumably his books henceforth had no more than a limited and clandestine circulation. They are preserved for us almost entirely in those few copies, made some time after his death, that found their way abroad.

Why was Courtenay so merciful? The question has been often debated with no very satisfactory outcome. The archbishop may have thought that the old man was broken—we do not know precisely when in 1382 he suffered his first stroke—and incapable of doing further harm. The difficulty about this explanation is that it assumes that Courtenay was deceived; for Wycliffe, ill though he might be, still had it in him to write some of his most cogent attacks on the Roman hierarchy. On the whole it is more probable that the compromise was the work of John of Gaunt. The evidence for this view is not decisive, but it at least fits in with Lancaster's reputation as the successful manager of a great affinity that he should have continued to defend a servant whose opinions he abhorred. When in the spring of 1384 the duke was the object of an unsuccessful attempt at assassination by an Irish Carmelite, it was in Wycliffe's view 'because he was unwilling to punish faithful priests' that the friars had plotted his death. This only proves that he was still regarded in a general way as the Lollards' protector, not that he was particularly responsible for Wycliffe's own immunity. But the second deduction is possible and Courtenay's otherwise inexplicable and uncharacteristic forbearance compels us to adopt it.

Whatever he might say about pledges of silence, Wycliffe took no great pains to avoid provocation in his writings. His later books were no more temperate in tone than their precursors; in the extravagance of their doctrine they far surpassed them. A trilogy, *On Simony, On Apostasy* and *On Blasphemy*, composed in 1381 and 1382, though in places it shows its author attempting to recover his allies by a parade of moderation, breaks out in its final chapters into the most uncompromising denunciation of every grade of the hierarchy from cardinals to door-keepers; priests and deacons alone had the sanction of the Gospels. Any clerk who received endowments greater than his bare needs was guilty of sin; so, too, was he who accepted fees in payment for baptising, marrying or bury-ing. It were better that all patronage should belong to laymen. Wycliffe defended at length his eucharistic teach-ing against objectors, gave a qualified approval to the practice of confession and condemned with Lutheran em-phasis the sale of indulgences. Repetitive and ill-arranged like most of his work, these three closely-connected books contain evidence of the speed with which his allies' deser-tion and the pressure of his enemies were driving him steadily to extremes. Having lost the support of the friars, he now described them as apostates and blasphemers with a special responsibility for spreading the heresy of transubstantiation, forgetful of the vows of poverty enjoined on them by their founders.

To 1382 also we must assign one of his most com-pendious and least ragged treatises, that which goes by the name of the *Trialogue*. This takes the form of a dis-cussion between Truth, Falsehood and Wisdom, and covers briefly but forcefully most of the subjects which he had dealt with at length elsewhere. It marks no obvious development in his opinions. The question of the Eucharist was evidently still causing him difficulty and although he is sure that transubstantiation is wrong he can do no better by way of positive definition than that the sacrament is 'the body of Christ in the form of bread'. The friars once more attract his keenest vituperation. The *Trialogue* was the first of his writings to be printed (at Basel in 1525) and provided therefore one of the few direct links between Wycliffe and the continental re-formers of the sixteenth century. In it, as in the last large-scale work on which he was engaged at the time of his death, the test by which all the institutions of the church were judged (and generally found wanting) was whether there were any authority for them in the Gospels somewhat literally interpreted. All else was in his eyes an unjustifiable accretion from which Christ's church should be freed; and both the papacy and the friars were included under that head.

If the Bible was the all-sufficient statement of God's law and if it was, as Wycliffe was hopeful enough to believe, perfectly intelligible by the simplest layman, then it followed that it ought to be made accessible to as many as possible by translation into English. The fact that some of the nobility owned French versions was no longer enough; many who could read could understand no other language than English. But the literate laity, important as they were, were not the only class to whom a vernacular Bible was likely to be welcome. It is doubtful how many of the inferior clergy had a sufficient knowledge of Latin to be able to make anything of the Vulgate; certainly not all. It may well be that the Lollards, when they undertook the production of an English translation, had them rather than the laity principally in mind.

What part Wycliffe himself played in it is as doubtful as so much else in his life. But the tendency of modern scholarship has been to reduce his share of the work to a minimum. He inspired it and he may have supervised it, but there is no reason to believe that he himself was responsible for a single sentence. That he ever wrote anything in the vernacular is open to question; his Latin works can in any case have left him with time for little else. Of the two complete Lollard translations of the Bible that have come down to us, one a literal and sometimes almost unintelligible crib, the other a free, accurate and idiomatic version, only the former was begun, as far as we know, in the master's life-time. There is good evidence for thinking that as far as verse 20 of the third chapter of the Book of Baruch it was made by, or more probably under the direction of, Nicholas Hereford. But the theory that he had reached this point in June 1382 when he was obliged to hurry off to Rome, though attractive, is much less well-founded, while it is quite uncertain which of the other Wycliffites took his place. It was presumably intended to enable a reader of weak Latinity to construe the Vulgate for himself. That it proved unsatisfactory for the Lollards' purposes is shown by the fact that it was soon replaced by the other and more readable version.

We know scarcely anything of the master's last years at Lutterworth, but we have no right therefore to assume that Wycliffe had belatedly turned his hand to his pastoral duties. To judge from the evidence of his literary output he can have rarely stirred from his desk. Nor is it easy to believe that the sermons that can with any certainty be ascribed to his pen were really ever intended for a non-academic congregation. Their author, it is true, calls them 'unpolished sermons for the people' and some of them contain allusions to events that occurred after he had withdrawn from Oxford. If their form was not merely a literary device, we can only hope that the yeomen and artisans of Lutterworth had not to sit under him too often. It is certain, however, that he employed a curate and that there were other clergy connected with the parish. The curate in 1384, by name John Horn, lived on for more than half a century to tell the story of his employer's death to the Oxford scholar Thomas Gascoigne in 1441. It is significant that Wycliffe was hearing mass and not celebrating it when he was smitten by his final illness.

The chief companion of his retirement was John Purvey, one of the most baffling figures in the Lollard movement. Ordained priest as of Lathbury near Newport Pagnell in 1377, Purvey may have been a member of the Buckinghamshire family who usually spelt their name Purefoy. Whereas one of our authorities calls him 'a most notable doctor' and speaks more than once of his great learning, he is never referred to as a graduate in any official document and the contemporary Leicester chronicler Knighton specifically describes him as 'a simple chaplain'. Until more definite evidence turns up it would be wise to exclude him from the list of Wycliffe's Oxford disciples. His great authority with the Lollards, though some came to distrust his lukewarmness, was derived from the fact, attested both by Knighton and Netter, that he was the amanuensis and inseparable Achates of their founder in his last days. It was probably he who was most responsible for the popular English expositions of Wycliffe's teaching, part translation, part adaptation of the Latin originals, which were circulating among the Lollards before the end of the century. His nickname of 'the Lollards' library' is thus best explained. As the vulgariser of the master's difficult scholastic arguments he seems to have stood midway between the Oxford followers like Hereford and Aston and such men as Swinderby. But he had not made himself notorious as a heretic until after Wycliffe's death.

This latter event is best told in the words of the octogenarian Horn: 'On Holy Innocents' Day [28 December 1384], as Wycliffe was hearing mass in his church at Lutterworth, just as the Host was elevated, he fell smitten by an acute paralysis, especially in the tongue so that neither then nor afterwards could he speak.' He lingered for three days and died on 31 December. Since for all that he had written and said he remained free from excommunication, he was buried in consecrated ground. It was not until long afterwards, when the general council of the Western Church, meeting at Constance, had condemned his teaching on something like three hundred counts, that his exhumation was ordered. By then, in 1415, Philip Repton was the bishop of the diocese in which Lutterworth lay and to his credit did nothing. It was only under Repton's successor, Richard Fleming, who had also once been suspected of Lollard opinions, that what were supposed to be the heresiarch's bones were dug up and burnt and the ashes cast into a nearby stream. This was in the spring of 1428.

Chapter Five

The Lollards, 1382–1413

WHILE Courtenay was scattering or suppressing the Oxford ringleaders, the diocesan in whose jurisdiction popular Lollardy was most notorious was making the up-country towns and villages almost as untenable by their chief local preacher. The bishop of Lincoln, John Buckingham, was himself no scholar, but one of the very few rank-and-file civil servants who in that period gained advancement to a see. His official acts prove him to have been a conscientious administrator of his unwieldy diocese. If he did not actually need the primate's example and exhortation to stir him to activity, yet it was not until the early months of 1382 that we have any evidence that he had begun to take effective measures against the heretic colony at Leicester. That at Lutterworth significantly escaped his notice altogether, so little were Wycliffe's parish and household a recognised source of heretical infection.

Since the beginning of the year the state of affairs at Leicester had become too open a scandal to be tolerated. The leading burgesses themselves were succumbing to the new doctrines. The Lenten season seems to have roused the little group at St. John's chapel, under the inspired leadership of Swinderby, to intenser activity. Alarmed by the reported success of William's evangelism, Buckingham on 5 March inhibited him from further preaching and cited him to appear forthwith before Mr. John Belvoir, the sub-dean of Lincoln, and a number of other judges in the prebendal church of Liddington in Rutland. The bishop's citation called in question the hermit's claim to the priesthood as well as his lack of an episcopal licence to preach. It had the effect of closing to him his usual haunts in churches and churchyards, but, ignoring the summons to trial, the Lollard then took to addressing the crowds that pressed to hear him from an improvised pulpit of mill-stones erected in the nearby highways. According to a very doubtful story, Leicester received a flying visit at this time from John Aston, but an offensive sermon said to have been preached by him on Palm Sunday (30 March) was in fact given by Swinderby himself. This was followed up by another on Good Friday (4 April) and perhaps several more, for which the congregation included the mayor and the more curious of the neighbouring clergy. The countenance given to Lollardy by the townsmen of Leicester and of some other midland boroughs is clearly borne out by the records.

The mendicant orders were not unnaturally alarmed by this too successful attempt to enter into competition with their own itinerant preachers and hastened to press on Buckingham the need for sterner measures. Swinderby's contumacious treatment of the latter's citation had already earned him excommunication, and a similar fate threatened those who participated in his illegal conventicles. But this does not seem to have daunted him. The next step was to summon him in the bishop's court to answer a charge of heresy; and sixteen articles based on his reported teaching were laid against him there by three friar masters of theology—a Franciscan, an Austin and a Dominican. On 12 May Buckingham, who was in London for parliament, committed the duty of investigating the case to two of his canons—the theologian Thomas Sutton and the lawyer Geoffrey Scrope. Once more the court which met at Lincoln on 9 June was kept waiting for the accused to appear. When, a few days later, he did, it is more than likely that force was employed to compel his attendance. His answer to the bishop's commissaries was a denial that he had ever believed, maintained, taught or publicly preached any of the opinions with which he was credited. The court, remembering his ill-repute, was disinclined to believe his professions, but gave him a month to clear himself by the evidence of twelve priests 'of good fame'. Meanwhile he was made to swear on the Gospels not to preach in future without an episcopal licence.

Buckingham had returned to Lincoln by 14 June when, after informing the clergy of the Leicester archdeaconry of what had occurred and having sent them a copy of the articles, he instructed them to cause all and sundry who were willing to speak against Swinderby at the time of his purgation to come forward and to denounce him. Any beneficed churchman who allowed the accused facilities for preaching rendered himself liable to excommunication. It is perhaps hardly surprising after this that Swinderby was unable to find the twelve clerical backers he needed.

Instead, when the day came, he produced a letter, attested by twelve seals, from the mayor and burgesses of Leicester to support his repeated denial of the doctrines of which he was accused. According to his own account, written down eight years later under the shadow of another trial, his final appearance before Buckingham, this time sitting in person with his commissaries, took place in the presence of the duke of Lancaster, the earl of Derby, Gaunt's fifteen-year-old heir, and many other magnates who were visiting Lincoln. What happened there may be given in the accused's own words:

'But when I should have made my purgation, there stood forth five friars and more, that some of them never saw me before nor heard me, and three lecherous priests openly known . . . that were there falsely forsworn, pursuing busily and crying with many another friar with great instance to give the doom upon me, to burn me and brought dry wood before, as men told in that town . . . with favour of the bishop, by what law I wot not, but soothly not by God's law. They said they held me as convicted and might not have forth my purgation. So as I fully forsook them [i.e. the opinions with which he was charged] and never granted that I said them, over this they made me to swear never to hold them, teach them nor preach them, privily nor apertly; and that I should go to certain churches to revoke the conclusions that I never said, in slander of myself, by great instance of the friars. And so for dread of death and [by] fleshly counsel that I had, I assented and so I did. And also they made me to swear that I should not preach, by instance of the friars, within [the] diocese without licence asked and granted.'

Swinderby's account of his trial, though he has confused the chronology a little, is borne out by the official record and the Leicester annalist. He was condemned to make a public recantation on successive Sundays during Mass in the cathedral of the diocese and in the parish churches where his errors had been disseminated. Buckingham's sentence is dated 11 July, from the chapter-house at Lincoln. On the following day he forwarded Archbishop Courtenay's general letter against the heretics to his parochial clergy.

If we may judge from Swinderby's behaviour in a later trial, his denials at Lincoln were based upon equivocations. Certainly, on a survey of his career as a whole, it is impossible to accept his plea that he was the innocent victim of the friars' malice. But there are significant differences between the opinions with which he was charged on 9 June and those which he was found guilty of holding on 11 July. Notably, the accusation of heretical teaching on the subject of the Real Presence was dropped. What were retained, though they owed something perhaps to Wycliffe's influence, were innocent of the master's later vagaries and, indeed, showed much more affinity with the puritan slogans that were soon to dominate the movement. Swinderby was found guilty of maintaining that a defaulting debtor should be allowed to go unpunished, that a man was justified in withholding tithes from a lecherous priest and that a state of sin in a minister invalidated the sacraments. It looks as if the denial of transubstantiation had been thrown in by mistake and was afterwards withdrawn or disproved.

Swinderby's reluctance to become a martyr cost him his popularity, it is said, with the devout puritans of Leicester. Not with all, however, for when on 15 September 1382 Thomas Beeby, one of the leading mercers of the town, a former mayor and member of parliament, came to make his will, he left forty shillings to William Swinderby, 'chaplain of the chapel of St. John at Leicester', but also a like amount to the house of the Franciscan friars. Beeby's attitude must have been exceptional, since the Lollard preacher decided to betake himself elsewhere. After a sojourn at Coventry, where his ministry again proved acceptable enough to provoke the bishop to action, he moved farther west across the Severn. Here he was soon to be joined by the remnants of the Oxford Wycliffites and to make new converts. His departure was followed by a period of peace at Leicester, though it seems that his former associates, Smith and Waytestathe, persisted in their old ways there, avoiding the publicity which was the breath of his life.

The days of publicity and immunity were nearly over. Henceforward the Lollard missionaries and their congregations were a persecuted sect, meeting in out-of-the-way places and often in secret, powerful in certain areas, apt to break out sporadically elsewhere, but only known to us when brought to light by the activities of some heresy-hunting bishop. The Lollards with whose exploits we are familiar were those who were careless or unlucky enough to be caught, the reluctant martyrs and those who shrank from martyrdom and once and for all abjured. They are met with only in the dock and the materials for the story of their church are the fragmentary, disjointed and, we may suppose, prejudiced records of some scores of judicial enquiries. Many of these records have not yet been printed, but even supposing that they all had been, the resulting distribution map of known Lollards might show only the incidence of those bishops willing or active to root them out. Between their trials the heretics disappear completely from our view. Their deaths, unless they were executed for their religion, are generally unrecorded. As for their organisation, if they had one, its story has died with them. Usually on the run, their leaders, it seems, often escaped capture and even their names are unknown. Their extensive vernacular writings are equally anonymous and most modern ascriptions as a rule baseless. After 1382, save for a few days in January 1414, Lollardy went to ground for ever; in so far as its adherents succeeded in evading their persecutors, they have also evaded us.

Darkness, however, did not immediately fall on those surviving members of Wycliffe's own circle who clung to his teaching. They were marked men from the first. Oxford knew them no more, but they soon found a refuge and a welcome together in the dioceses of Hereford and Worcester and along the marches of South Wales. This was John Aston's own country and the concentration of the Lollards there was probably due to his influence. There may also have been something in the revivalism of the missionaries which made an appeal to the submerged Welsh. Aston's recantation at Oxford in November 1382, if it came from the heart, was certainly not lasting. On 21 September 1383 he preached a sermon at Gloucester against the bishop of Norwich's 'crusade' to convert the Flemish supporters of the anti-pope by force of arms. This by itself would have been no clear evidence of a relapse. Quite a number of sound Catholics doubted the merits of that filibustering adventure—especially after it had failed. But some of Aston's recorded statements on this occasion were tainted and before long he was undoubtedly consorting with other heretics.

It was natural that Nicholas Hereford, when he returned from abroad late in 1385, should make his way also to the west from which he sprang. His senseless journey to Rome had ended disastrously, but he had not yet quite learnt his lesson. He had nursed the idea that he might be able to win Urban VI's support for the Lollards and persuade him to reverse Courtenay's judgement and excommunication. Very reasonably he was arrested and condemned anew by the scandalised cardinals. It is said that but for the pope's clemency he would have suffered death in Rome for his pains; instead, he was thrown into prison. From what might have been life-long captivity he was rescued by a popular rising—this was most likely one which is known to have occurred in June 1385—in which the prisons were raided and their inmates indiscriminately freed. Hereford succeeded in making good his escape home to England. Here he lay low for a time, where is uncertain, but near enough to Worcester to annoy its bishop. He would have been wiser had he stayed safely west of Severn.

Bristol became Purvey's refuge after Wycliffe's death. The fact that, like Oxford, it lay on the borders between two dioceses (those of Worcester and Wells) seems to account for its comparative immunity from episcopal intervention. This deprives us of any detailed evidence about what was soon to become, thanks to Purvey's labours, one of the chief urban centres of Lollard influence. The hinterland of small cloth-weaving towns and prosperous villages to which Bristol served as port was one of the richest areas in the country. Its artisans, encouraged by financial independence and a little book-learning, proved sympathetic to the new ideas. The effectiveness of Purvey's sermons, which he delivered clad like an ordinary layman with what an enemy mocked at as a display of saintliness beyond his fellows, is well attested. But it is said that at first Hereford assumed the leadership among Wycliffe's surviving disciples.

For a time their ministrations were discreet enough to escape episcopal notice, but on 10 August 1387 the bishop of Worcester, Henry Wakefield, prohibited five Lollards by name and any others like them from preaching in his diocese. The five offenders, about whom Wakefield was none too well informed, were the two doctors, Hereford and Aston, and their inferior colleagues, Purvey, John Parker (who is not otherwise known) and Swinderby. The order was probably that of their reputed importance, but Hereford was, in fact, already a prisoner. This proclamation is not known to have had any effect. It was followed during 1388 and 1389 by a series of royal commissions, appointed at the instance of the parliament of March 1388, to confiscate the works of Wycliffe, Hereford, Aston and Purvey and to arrest their possessors. About the same time Richard Lavenham, prior of the Carmelite house in Bristol, began to make a collection of Purvey's heresies. Wakefield, however, was slow to move.

So although the hue and cry was thus for a time raised

against them, the majority of the Lollard leaders continued at large. John Aston almost certainly died in or soon after 1388. According to an admirer who wrote twenty years later, he remained of Wycliffe's faith to the end; and he was not the man to have been inactive. Hereford was the first casualty. Venturing too far afield, he was arrested in Nottingham and committed to the town gaol there early in 1387. On 1 February the government had been apprised and ordered the civic authorities to hand him over to the constable of Nottingham castle. A number of townsmen who were detected owning heretical books were also imprisoned and those of them that remained 'obstinate with hardened minds' were next year summoned to answer before the king's council. What happened thereafter remains obscure, but it is likely that Hereford was handed over to Courtenay's keeping, since it was in response to the primate's information that his arrest had been ordered. His fellow-Lollards believed that he was 'grievously tormented' while in Courtenay's hands, but doubtless they were at a loss to explain otherwise what now befell.

It cannot have been long before Hereford saw the desirability of submission and had succeeded in gaining influential patronage for his apostasy. This must have happened some time before 12 December 1391. On that day he was granted the king's protection by advice of the council on the somewhat unlikely ground that, because of 'his zeal in preaching privately and openly in opposition to false teachers who subverted the Catholic faith', his discomfited enemies were suing him maliciously in the courts in an effort to silence him. October 1393 saw him back in his native Herefordshire, acting as one of the bishop's assessors in a Lollard's trial. It cannot have surprised him to receive an open letter from one of his former associates, reproaching him as a turncoat and, less pointedly, for his weak Latin grammar and worse pronunciation. His promotion by the crown to the chancellorship of Hereford cathedral on 16 February 1394 may have done a little to soothe his feelings. It was supplemented by other pieces of preferment during the next few years. He remained a target for Lollard malice, but was obviously quite capable of keeping his own end up when it came to debate. As he was once heard to boast, it gave him 'more delight to hold against them than ever he had to hold with them'. Royal favours made his ways pleasant; after Richard II had endowed him liberally with fuel from the king's woods, Henry IV capped this gift with an annual barrel of wine. Still Master Nicholas was not content. Many years later, in 1417, he threw up everything—benefices and doles—to retire to die in extreme old age, an inmate of the Carthusian monastery of St. Anne at Coventry. One would gladly know more of this gifted, sanguine and erratic scholar.

Swinderby's turn came next. On 10 November 1388 the sheriff of Herefordshire was ordered to arrest him and hand him over to the bishop, John Gilbert, or to his ministers (for the bishop was, in fact, treasurer of England and fully occupied at Westminster). No action seems to have resulted before Gilbert was translated to St. David's in the following May, but a copy of the proceedings before Buckingham in 1382 was filed by the authorities at Hereford in readiness for his trial. Swinderby had recanted and gone back on his recantation; he was a lapsed heretic and could expect to fare ill if laid by the heels. But that did not discourage him from great preaching activity in various parts of the diocese during the next two years.

Gilbert's successor in the see was John Trefnant, an undoubtedly conscientious but slow-moving disciplinarian, whose denunciation of heresy was received and read by Swinderby at Monmouth some time in 1390. This is the most southerly place at which the Lollard is recorded, his normal range having been, it seems, along the western borders of Herefordshire north from Clifford, Eardisley and Almeley to Wigmore and Kington, from which places it was easy for him to slip out of the diocese into the safety of the Welsh hills. On Monday, 1 August 1390, for example, he preached a sermon at Whitney-on-Wye that gave sad offence to the rector of nearby Kinnersley who happened to hear him; and on 8 September following he celebrated mass in what the bishop described as an unconsecrated chapel in the park at Newton near Leintwardine. The site of yet another of his reputed haunts, 'a chapel not hallowed but a cursed shepherd's hut' in 'a desert wood clept Derwald's Wood', cannot now be identified. On one occasion he had the hardihood to appear uninvited to have speech with Trefnant at Pembridge.

Although it is clear that the bishop acted with reluctance, Swinderby was at length summoned to hear the charges laid against him at Kington on 14 June 1391. He was given until the last day of the month to prepare his reply. There are signs that he had powerful friends among the gentry of the diocese, for it was at their request that Trefnant granted him a safe-conduct: if he came before his judges at Bodenham church on the appointed day he should be free to depart again without arrest. Accordingly, on 30 June he put in an appearance, submitted a long paper defence—he seems to have had unexpected misgivings about making a verbal rejoinder—and then withdrew again into hiding. His case was that he had been falsely and maliciously charged with heresy at Lincoln, and that he had then admitted his guilt and done penance to avoid the fire that had been illegally prepared for him. But his detailed answers on the subject of the eleven 'conclusions' with which he had been credited by Buckingham amounted to little more than a succession of clever, indeed quibbling, evasions. Each was supported by a brief selection of authorities, biblical and patristic.

If Swinderby was typical of the rank and file of unbeneficed and poorly-paid clergy without a university education on whom fell the burden of parochial work in those days, then the class cannot be dismissed as thoughtless or unread. The trial at Bodenham was not concerned directly with what had already been abjured nine years before. What Swinderby had now to answer was that notwithstanding his recantation of 1382 he had presumed once more to preach false doctrine in another diocese. Fifteen articles of accusation had been drawn up, based upon the evidence of those who had heard him at Whitney and Newton. His method of dealing with them was first of all to deny that he had ever said what was alleged against him: 'I never thought this, nor spake this, nor preached this nor heard this to the time that I saw it written in our book [i.e. the list of articles against him]; and then to spoil the effect of the denial by giving the gist of what he had actually said, words that were in themselves erroneous enough to secure his conviction.

The counts on which he was tried, apart from his having celebrated mass in unhallowed buildings, were similar in many cases to those on which Buckingham's court had found him guilty: that sin excommunicates the sinner without the need for a prelate, that 'outward confession by word is superfluous' for the truly contrite, that all priests have equal power be they pope or curate, that papal indulgences are vain, that the celebrant who is in mortal sin cannot 'by the strength of the sacramental words make God's body' and that those who worship 'the image of Him that was done on the cross' are guilty of idolatry. But it is interesting to find that charges which had been dropped or dismissed at Lincoln were revived. Thus he was accused of denying transubstantiation, of believing 'that in the sacrament of God's body is not very [i.e. truly] God's body' and of affirming 'that material bread lives there with God's body in the same sacrament'. And once more these were the charges to which he returned unqualified denials: 'this I said never, God wot' and 'this conclusion have I not holden, nor taught nor preached, for I have not meddled me of that matter, my wit sufficeth not thereto'.

Thereafter the bishop had some difficulty in luring the suspect from his hiding-place. A series of citations throughout the summer drew blank, though one of them caused Swinderby to return a characteristic answer in writing:

'I marvel why ye have sent out so sharp letters for me. . . . I beseech you meekly that you have me excused of my coming to Ledbury; for it is certified me by my friends that I have many enemies that lie in wait for me, and also it is told me that the king's commission

is come for me and cried in towns, and bailiffs charged
to take me if they may and put me in prison. And I
know the frailness of myself and seeing how Peter, that
much loved Christ, forsook Him for dread, and many
great clerks for duress of prison have fallen away from
truth and some well-nigh lost their wits, and wherefore
also I dread to come . . . I pray you . . . have pity on me.
And if ye come nigh me where . . . I durst well come to
you, I will be ready to come to you without summons to
take your information after Christ's love. Or if ye have
found in my confession any many errors against Christ's
teaching I will beseech you meekly to send it me written
—as I sent you at your commandment my confession
written—and if I see that I have erred against God's
law I will be amended by you as I have said you here-
before. Christ, that is prince of shepherds, keep you
from evil and bring you to bliss.'

One wonders how Trefnant enjoyed being treated with
such familiar equality by the man he described as 'a pre-
tended priest'. He certainly made no attempt to join
Swinderby in the marches, and when at length the accused
was induced to present himself for judgement on 3 October it was to Hereford that he had to come. Although he
had been pronounced contumacious, he was not cowed.
He and his supporters had already put in a curious document which endeavoured to prove that a priest was lawfully entitled to preach in any diocese without its bishop's
leave. Now, when he made his last personal appearance
before his judges, he offered once again a written defence
of his views. This was a lively composition, thoroughly
typical of the man. Despite his initial claim that he was
'but simply lettered' and knew no sophisms, he told the
bishop that although his conclusions had been found
erroneous and heretical, yet he could 'see none error in
them'; and he went on to justify his teaching on the withholding of tithe, the remission of sin, the Eucharist, the
papacy and Despenser's 'crusade'. He denied the pope's
ability to grant indulgences; 'but if any man can show me
that he have such a power grounded in the truth of holy

writ, I will gladly leave it'. Of the friars he asked the question: 'Might not men lawfully take from them such lordships and make them to live in poverty, as their rule would?' On the sacrament of the altar alone he was reticent; it was both 'bread and Christ's body', but he did not venture to be more explicit.

Before the court pronounced judgement he had again withdrawn to safety, though it is not clear whether he did so by or without the bishop's leave. After so brazen a stand against authority his condemnation was inevitable, and it is difficult to understand why he should have made a grievance of the fact that it was passed on him in his absence. Trefnant found him to be 'a heretic, a schismatic, a false informer and seducer of the people and as such to be avoided by those faithful to Christ'. On his failure to come for correction, he was excommunicated. When he heard this he appealed, not to a higher ecclesiastical tribunal but to the king's justices in parliament, and sent his conclusions 'to the knights of the parliament to be shewed to the lords'. Addressing the commons as 'dear, worshipful sirs in this world', he waxed very eloquent for their benefit:

> 'As we see by many tokens that this world draws to an end and all that ever have been forth brought of Adam kind into this world shall come together at doomsday . . . therefore be ye stable and true to God. . . . This land is full of ghostly [i.e. spiritual] cowardice, in ghostly battle few do stand. But Christ the comforter of all . . . barks for our love against the fiend. That doughty Duke comforteth us thus: "Be ye strong in battle", He says, "and fight ye with the old adder". Awake, ye that be righteous men!'; and so on down to the signature from 'a poor liege man of the king's and your poor priest, William of Swinderby'.

No chronicler mentions whether this open letter reached its destination; nor is there any record that parliament considered it. Swinderby's reliance upon the king's justice was not well-grounded. Richard II, who had emerged from his minority in 1389, was a devout, almost passionately loyal, son of the church with no wish to tolerate heretics. But it may have been the fear of trouble in parliament that made Trefnant submit the opinions of the convicted Lollard to a group of Cambridge theologians for reasoned scrutiny. As was to be expected, they found them damnable.

Swinderby did not allow his expectation of royal favour to make him careless of his personal safety. Not long after his trial he betook himself with one faithful companion, Stephen Bell, a literate and, it seems, a layman, into Wales. Trefnant, who heard that he was still lurking in the neighbourhood as late as January 1392, applied on 12 February for the king's authority to arrest and imprison him and Bell wherever they could be found, even if it were beyond the bounds of the diocese of Hereford. Richard, when granting this petition on 9 March, instructed his local officials to bring the fugitives before him in his council if they refused to obey the commands of Holy Church. Proclamation was to be made that anyone who harboured them or concealed their whereabouts was liable to forfeit all his goods. The crown was behind Trefnant, but it is pleasant to record that the two Lollards were never given up. They, 'their abettors and accomplices' disappeared for ever into the wilds, where history cannot follow them.

Swinderby's life and trials are worth dwelling on. Not only did his teaching come closer to the beliefs of the humble Lollards of the fifteenth century, the 'Bible men' as an opponent called them, than did much of Wycliffe's more difficult theology, but he was personally—and, as far as we know, solely—responsible for making many converts, some of them important ones, in a new area. Not the least of those whose hearts were first touched by his fervour, it is almost certain, was the son and heir of the squire of Almeley, John Oldcastle by name, a boy then in his teens who, a quarter of a century later, became Lollardy's foremost martyr. If Swinderby had done no other service to the movement, he would deserve to be remembered for this. But the importance of his share in its foundation has never been justly appreciated. Not that he did not owe much to Wycliffe, or at least to Wycliffe's circle, but among those who made the master's doctrines intelligible to the unlearned, while adding much of his own simplicity as well, he has a claim to a high place. Above all, he was one of the greatest, perhaps the very greatest, of Lollard evangelists. Wherever he preached he gained followers, in the market towns of Leicestershire as well as among the hills and valleys between Clun Forest and the Black Mountain. The records of his second trial, luckily preserved for us by Trefnant's industrious registrar, leave no doubt that he had gained a dangerous hold over the border district. In the earnest puritanism, the unself-conscious arrogance, the rhetoric and the equivocation of his surviving utterances, the man's power is vividly revealed. This 'simple priest', who boasted that he had no use for sophistry and yet took pleasure in chopping logic with his bishop, was quite as subversive of order as the authorities believed.

Trefnant did manage to bring one of the Lollard's flock to justice, namely, Walter Brute, who described himself as 'sinner, layman, husbandman and Christian'. Whence he gained his very considerable knowledge of Latin and his facility in dialectic is somewhat mysterious; though not in orders, he may have been a graduate of Oxford. The fact that he did not follow Swinderby into the wilderness suggests that he had more of a stake in the county than his migrant leader. Yet he had long evaded citations from both Archbishop Courtenay and Bishop Gilbert to answer a charge of heresy. It is not clear how he was caught in 1391, but on 15 October in that year, scarcely a fortnight after Swinderby's condemnation, he appeared before the precentor, Walter Ramsbury, and several members of the chapter as well as 'certain other credible witnesses' in the house of one of the canons at Hereford. There he asserted that the judgement against Swinderby had been erroneous and that the condemned opinions had been true and catholic. In addition he is alleged to have maintained that the Host remained bread after consecration and that the pope was without any doubt antichrist, views quite compatible with his having attended Wycliffe's lectures at Oxford.

One would have thought that such utterances would have been enough to ensure his immediate conviction, but Trefnant was conscientious to a fault. It was not until the following 19 January that Brute was induced to come to the bishop's manor-house of Whitbourne for cross-examination. There, in Trefnant's presence, he affirmed that Christians were not bound to pay tithes and that all oaths were unlawful. More serious was his admission that he had that very month taken meat and drink with Swinderby, the excommunicated fugitive from justice. Thereupon a number of clergy, headed by Walter Pride, penitentiary of Hereford, formally charged Brute with a series of heresies before the bishop in the nearby parish church. The accused then as usual became elusive and the judge slighted but persistent. Times and places for trial were again and again fixed. Brute sometimes appeared in person, sometimes by proxy, and in reply to Trefnant's demand set out his ideas in Latin in a series of apocalyptic essays. The first and shortest proceeded from two suppositions to two conclusions: if the pope legislated against Christ's gospel, he was 'the idol of desolation sitting in the temple of God', and if the city of Rome approved his traditions, then it was Babylon, 'the great whore sitting upon many waters'. These were supported by strings of not very intelligible quotations from scripture. Brute claimed that both his parents were Britons, as he called Welshmen. His oratorical style and his fondness for the language of *Revelation* bear him out. He was evidently a fellow-countryman of Owen Glendower.

It was less surprising that Trefnant complained of his obscurity than that he asked for more. The result was a spate of heresy on every sort of subject. In his reliance upon grace as well as by his rejection of transubstantiation Brute was clearly Wycliffe's pupil, but his cloudy grandiloquence was his own. Not even John Foxe, who thought almost any utterance by a heretic worthy of a place in his *Book of Martyrs,* could be bothered to quote all of Brute's.

Still, perhaps their verbosity had its point. The time that was wasted in their composition and in their solemn examination by an absurdly large body of doctors, headed by John Necton, chancellor of Cambridge, and including Adam Usk the chronicler and Hereford the turncoat, at least spun out the proceedings until the autumn of 1393. Then, when Trefnant was at last ready to pronounce judgement and had once more summoned the accused to appear in person before him and his assessors in Hereford cathedral on 3 October, he learnt that he might find his authority frustrated by an appeal to violence. Brute and his 'accomplices' were reported to have formed an armed conspiracy to prevent the execution of the bishop's sentence. On 22 September, therefore, the king ordered proclamation to be made against those forming 'conventicles, assemblies or confederacies by any colour . . . whereby . . . the said bishop and doctors might be by any means molested . . . in the carrying out of such correction as should be done in accordance with' the church's law. To make this effective, a commission of knights and others was ordered to arrest and bring before the king's council such as should disobey it. Thus safeguarded, the court met on Friday, 3 October, and the two following days. Brute, who had surrendered himself for judgement, was in a chastened mood. On the Sunday he produced a scroll written in English as follows:

> 'I, Walter Brute, submit me principally to the evangel of Jesus Christ and to the determination of holy church, to the general councils of holy church and to the sentence and determination of the four doctors of holy writ, that is Augustine, Ambrose, Jerome and Gregory; and I meekly submit me to your correction as a subject ought to his bishop.'

This contented Trefnant, who merely ordered him to recite it in a loud and intelligible voice on the morrow at the cross in the cathedral yard. And this was duly done in the presence of the bishop, his assessors, barons, knights, gentry, clergy and people. The warden of New College,

Oxford, Thomas Cranley, improved the occasion with a sermon on the text: *Be not highminded, but fear* (Rom. xi, 20). It was a lesson that the penitent Brute did not altogether take to heart, since he rose with Owen Glendower against the English and met his death in the lost cause of Welsh independence. But no more is heard of overt Lollardy for a time in the diocese of Hereford.

Compared with the Welsh border, London contributed little at this date to the history of dissent. Favourable though its urban soil was at other times to the spread of new religious movements, its bishop was, in fact, less troubled than either Buckingham or Trefnant. Strife there was, bitter and prolonged, but it had almost nothing to do with Wycliffe and left the citizens with scarcely any time to imbibe the Lollards' teaching. Its origins were social and of long standing: the hatred of the smaller merchants and tradesmen for the narrow oligarchy of would-be monopolists that controlled the city's government. Brought into the open at the time of the Good Parliament, this hostility was never far below the surface throughout the ensuing decade. For a time John Northampton, a rich mercer who enjoyed the patronage of John of Gaunt, succeeded in making himself the political 'boss' of London. But his rule was short and ultimately the old order was restored. Like the shrewd demagogue that he was, he played for the support of the puritan bourgeoisie by shaving the heads of the city's harlots and promoting sterner measures against usury. Nothing could have been more orthodox than this. Yet, from a curious treatise which his secretary, Thomas Usk, later wrote in prison, it appears that some, at least, of his supporters were tainted with Lollardy. They do not seem to have been either influential or active. But it is probable that the temper of the Londoners was hostile to authority and therefore disposed to anti-clericalism.

This, rather than the prevalence of genuine Lollardy, seems to be the explanation of a curious incident which occurred in 1387 and was grossly exaggerated by the St. Albans chronicler. An Austin friar called either Peter or William Pattishall had bought a papal chaplaincy from an itinerant salesman of such honours. This, says Walsingham, turned his head and caused him to join the Wycliffites. All that he seems to have done, in fact, was to accuse his brethren of a variety of crimes from the pulpit of St. Christopher's-by-the-Stocks. When the London Austins challenged his facts a riot ensued. The 'Lollards' (there were 'almost a hundred' of them, according to the chronicle) cried out: 'Let us rout these murderers, burn these sodomites, hang these traitors'; but an attempt to burn the friars' houses was thwarted by the prompt intervention of a sheriff. Pattishall then nailed his charges to the door of St. Paul's, thanking God that he had escaped from the company of such wicked and impure men. The story ends with an order for his arrest which is dated 18 July 1387. In spite of Walsingham's assertions to the contrary, there is really no certain evidence of Lollardy here. Wycliffe had had Austin friends, it is true, but there is nothing to connect him with Pattishall's troubles or the London house.

What makes it difficult to believe that the capital was a notorious haunt of Lollards is the absence of any move by the ecclesiastical authorities to subject it to disciplinary visitation. Had the diocesan Braybrooke hesitated, the vigilant Courtenay would almost certainly have intervened. The fact that he did so only once, in the case of a layman called Nicholas Ipswich, makes it probable that whatever heretics lurked in the city or its suburbs their activities were limited enough to escape notice.

The archbishop intervened, for example, at Leicester. Buckingham was content to have driven Swinderby from his diocese; he did not trouble to deal with the other occupants of St. John's chapel. Their peace was broken by the arrival of Courtenay at St. Mary's abbey, Leicester, on 30 October 1389, in the course of a metropolitical visitation of the Lincoln diocese. Eight of them were at once denounced by the well-affected inhabitants of the town as notorious teachers of heresy and a selection of their opinions was, as usual, submitted. In addition to Smith and Waytestathe, those accused included a Scrivener, a Parchmener, a Taylor and a Goldsmith, names that provide a clue to their occupations and social status. It was said of them that they favoured consubstantiation and lay preaching and were opposed to indulgences, enforced confession, the veneration of images and the unconditional payment of tithes and other customary dues. When the archbishop cited them to appear before him in the abbey on All Saints' Day, Monday, 1 November, they hid themselves, 'desiring to walk in darkness rather than in light'. Thereupon Courtenay, having celebrated high mass at the great altar of St. Mary's, with solemnity excommunicated all and sundry who then or thereafter held such opinions or taught them. Early next morning a committee of local worthies, priests and laymen, deposed on oath that it was notorious in Leicester and in other places round about that the eight accused were guilty. They were then excommunicated by name. An anchoress called Maud, who inhabited a cell in the churchyard of St. Peter's, Leicester, was next examined by Courtenay's emissaries and, her answers being found sophistical, was summoned to appear before him on 6 November at Northampton. She came, submitted and was allowed to resume her dedicated life.

Excommunication having failed to cow Smith and his fellows, Courtenay wrote from Towcester on the 7th ordering the civic magistrates of Leicester to see to their arrest. Ten days later three of them, of whom Smith was one, were brought to make their submission at Dorchester-on-Thames. It was held particularly against Smith that he and Waytestathe had taken a wooden statue of St. Katherine and burnt it for fuel. He was also said to have referred to two famous images of the Virgin as 'the witch of Lincoln' and 'the witch of Walsingham' respectively. His fellow-prisoners, a married couple named Dexter, though less iconoclastic, had apparently refused to venerate the crucified Christ. All three hastened to abjure their errors and were condemned to do appropriate penance. The archbishop's charity was displayed by the concession that on account of the November weather the penitents should be relieved of the necessity of stripping to their shifts. Apart from this, their humiliation in the market-place of Leicester was to be public and complete. The

literate Smith, who was said to have spent eight years com-
piling English books based upon the New Testament and
the writings of the Fathers, was made to surrender them
to his judge. Had they survived, they might have given
us a better notion of the capacities of this self-educated
blacksmith. As it is, he is scarcely a recognisable person,
though the type is familiar enough from the later annals
of English nonconformity.

Northampton was also subjected to official visitation by
Courtenay in 1389, but without the discovery of any
Lollard congregations there. Yet within three years it had
almost outdistanced Leicester as a notorious centre of
heresy, thanks, it was alleged, to the protection and encouragement of John Fox, who was elected mayor in the
autumn of 1392. For our knowledge of what happened
between Christmas and Easter following—once more Lent
provided an occasion for Lollard excesses—we are entirely
dependent upon an information laid against Fox and his
adherents by a fellow-townsman and wool-merchant called
Richard Stormsworth. This told how 'the first maintainer
of Lollardy in Northampton', James Collin, a runaway
mercer's apprentice from London, had been received into
the mayor's household. Fox was easily persuaded to invite
others of the sect to visit him, so that his house soon
became an asylum for a motley collection of heretics.
Here were to be found Richard Bullock, chaplain, whom
the archdeacon of Northampton had already convicted of
false doctrine, Thomas Compworth (or perhaps Comber-
worth), who had suffered the same fate at the hands of
the chancellor and doctors of Oxford, Nicholas Weston, an
apostate Carmelite friar, and a couple of other Lollard
preachers. Most prominent, however, was the singular
figure of Mr. William Northwold who, according to
Stormsworth, had occupied the archdeaconry of Sudbury
for about seven years,

'and at his departure from the same took a great sum of
money by way of simony, on which he liveth deliciously
at this time in the house of St. Andrew at Northampton,
where he hath caused such debate between the prior and

monks that the house is wellnigh undone, and many of
the monks fled away'.

This had happened at other houses in which Northwold
had previously lodged. 'His whole conversation,' adds
Stormsworth,

'as well in the court of Rome as in England hath been in
simony and subtle dealing, who notwithstanding is still in
Northampton amongst the Lollards and misbelievers reputed a prophet speaking with the tongue of an angel.'

Although Friar Weston was intruded by the mayor into
a curacy at St. Gregory's, the church of All Saints' and the
market cross adjoining it seem to have been the chief
scenes of Lollard demonstrations which began on
26 December, 1392, led to a breach of the peace on
Sunday, 12 January, and reached a climax on 9 March,
when Bishop Buckingham's commissioners were rated and
defied by Fox and Northwold. Messengers had been sent
to Oxford and elsewhere to hire preachers of the word,
and these, in order 'to be reputed of the common people
for great clerks', dressed themselves up in gowns and hoods
to which they were not entitled. Northwold appeared in
the guise of a doctor of divinity, 'whereas he never took
any degree in schools'. Stormsworth claims that he tried to
stop one Lollard from preaching and was nearly lynched
for his pains, that he was thereupon indicted for causing
the affray, found guilty by a packed jury of Fox's supporters in his absence and prevented by the mayor from
obtaining redress: 'no action is there maintainable by the
inhabitants against the Lollards during this man's
mayoralty'. Recourse was on that account necessary to the
king's council.

How much of this lively and circumstantial story can
we believe? For what the petitioner said about Northwold's shady past there is a good deal of supporting
evidence in the records; but though the allegation of
simony in England and Rome may have been true, there
was nothing specifically Lollard in that. The case against

Thomas Compworth was far stronger, indeed damning. An esquire of Kidlington near Oxford who, men said, had run about the country preaching heresy for years, he had been brought to trial in 1385 for refusing tithe to the rector of his parish, the abbot of Oseney. Imprisoned in Banbury castle, he was charged before a bench of Oxford doctors presided over by the chancellor, to whom Courtenay and Buckingham committed the hearing. The court found him guilty of various heresies and errors, enforced his submission and condemned him to pay the injured abbot £40. Only a convenient illness saved him from a more public humiliation. Compworth had Northamptonshire affiliations and these may have caused him to enjoy Fox's patronage.

About the mayor's other associates there is much less evidence. One of them may have been John Stoke, parson of Widmerpool, who had been in Nottingham gaol in 1389 under suspicion of heresy. But Friar Weston had only recently been made a papal chaplain. Fox himself was, of course, a well-known and prosperous member of the Northampton bourgeoisie. He had represented the town in parliament and in 1392–3 was serving his third term as its mayor. Like Stormsworth he was a woolman and that, perhaps, was the source of the trouble between them. For Stormsworth was far from being the innocent, disinterested informer that his petition suggested. He had, in fact, been charged once before with uttering threats against a fellow-townsman. When he composed his long indictment of Fox's rule, he had only recently been tried in the latter's court for failing to use standard weights and measures and found guilty. An appeal against this verdict was pending before the king's council in April 1393. He was thus a man with a personal grievance, if not a grudge; and this cannot but weaken the value of his testimony. Even so, it is difficult to believe that he did not choose the ground that was most likely to give him firm support against his opponent. He may have exaggerated wildly, but it is improbable that he invented the whole series of incidents he described.

And so the government evidently thought. For on

24 April 1393 Fox was dismissed from the mayoralty and the men of Northampton were told to choose his successor. Their protest, dated four days later, that Stormsworth's charges were malicious and the late mayor's rule orderly and acceptable seems to have had no effect. Fox was arrested and sent to Nottingham castle, to be kept there in custody until further notice. At first Stormsworth so far succeeded in imposing on the king that he was able to obtain letters under the signet ordering the lawless borough to make him mayor in Fox's place. But by the autumn the council had discovered that he was quite unsuitable and instructed the burgesses to elect freely, provided that their choice fell on 'no man impeached or defamed for evil opinions and unsound doctrine'.

Little else is known of this affair save that Bishop Buckingham was worrying about heresy at Northampton in August 1393 and that on 9 November 1394 he applied for the arrest of five Lollards of the town, of whom one, at least, the chaplain Richard Bullock, was mentioned in Stormsworth's petition. The borough once more elected Fox mayor in September 1395, only to be forbidden to admit him by the king. But Henry of Lancaster was his patron and in 1399 a new reign saw him holding office for a fourth time. His orthodoxy was not again questioned, a fact that suggests his lapse was at best only temporary. Northwold was less lucky; in 1397 he was given strict orders by the king, on pain of imprisonment and forfeiture, to abstain from teaching and preaching within the realm, either secretly or openly, in future. It is clear that Mr. William Northwold, ex-archdeacon and sower of discord in monastic houses, was unwise enough to mix a little too much high thinking with his delicious living; that, in short, he was a Lollard, if not of a common sort.

Wycliffe's teaching, therefore, in the decade after his death had found a welcome in many widely-separated areas. Persecution had helped to scatter it in town and country. Those in authority can easily be forgiven for thinking that it might spring up anywhere and in any social class. Apart from the first Oxford disciples, the converts were, with few exceptions, of humble birth and little formal education: chaplains, townsmen, small free-holders and skilled craftsmen, self-taught, serious-minded, opinionated people. From its early days the movement had its usual complement of devout women, though none ever attained importance in it. The Lollards had no Vittoria Colonna, no Selina countess of Huntingdon, not even a Mary Magdalen. If some of them believed a priest-hood to be without scriptural warrant and hence undesir-able, their leaders were nevertheless men. So, too, were such patrons as they succeeded in winning among the greater land-owners. No lady of gentle birth is known to have displayed any sympathy for the hunted missionaries, still less to have embraced their creed. There is nothing to suggest that the wife of Sir John Oldcastle himself was anything but indifferent to the opinions for which her husband died.

Oldcastle's sincerity is beyond question. That of Thomas Compworth may be presumed. But there is more reason to doubt that of the Lollards' many other reputed protectors among the landed gentry. The chroniclers are responsible for the belief, nowadays too often rejected, that the preachers could depend upon the favour and even the outright adherence of an active group of knights, including some attached to the royal household. Various lists of these military Lollards who 'were the most strenuous pro-moters and doughtiest champions of that sect' are given by Knighton and Walsingham. But the careers of some of those named must tend to shake one's faith in the chroni-clers' assertion. Not heretics conceivably, it is hard to suppose that they were even anti-clericals. Only the ex-cited gossip of the abbeys connects them with subversive agitation. Two of them, for example, met their deaths near Constantinople on an expedition that was either a crusade or a pilgrimage; whichever it may have been, it was not an activity commended by Lollards. It is just possible that some of them may at an early stage have been favourable to disendowment and then have dropped the policy when it became dangerous or discredited. But their lives, their connections and, above all, their recorded sup-port of practices the Lollards savagely denounced make it absurd to believe that they were thorough-going heretics for long, if, indeed, at all.

Lollard knights, however, there certainly were. Chroniclers were often unreliable, but they rarely concocted a story without genuine ingredients. Of those they named, one was without any doubt inclined to heresy and the company of heretics, and three others are at least gravely suspect. Sir Thomas Latimer, a wealthy midland landowner whose seat was at Braybrooke in Northamptonshire, is known to have possessed heretical books and pamphlets when in 1388 he was summoned before the council for examination. Next year he was in still more serious trouble for protecting a Lollard chaplain called John Woodward who had made many converts (forty-five are named) in south-west Northamptonshire from Latimer's manor of Chipping Warden. Braybrooke itself became a resort of Lollards. Its rector (and Latimer owned the advowson), Robert Hook, first got into ill odour for teaching and writing heresy in 1405, but remained an active Lollard there for another twenty years. In 1414 a certain Thomas Ile of Braybrooke was accused of being a writer and distributor of heretical tracts, and it was at Braybrooke in or shortly before 1407 that two visiting Czech scholars copied a manuscript of Wycliffe's treatise *On Lordship* to send home to Prague. The suspicion under which Latimer fell would seem to have been abundantly justified. That he was not proceeded against more vigorously must be ascribed to his rank and long military service. He died in 1401, when even those might not have saved him much longer.

The guilt of Sir John Montagu, who in 1397 succeeded to the earldom of Salisbury, Sir Lewis Clifford and Sir John Cheyne, though much less well authenticated, is also hard to dismiss out of hand. The most damaging count against Clifford and Cheyne was their close association with Latimer; and all three men made notably similar wills expressing their self-contempt and contrition in unusually strong terms. Montagu, for political reasons the most hated of the suspects, is said to have removed the images from his chapel at Shenley in Hertfordshire and to have offered a refuge there to Nicholas Hereford and other Lollard preachers. But there is no real ground for thinking that his unorthodoxy long survived 1387. His hold on the king's affections was increasing and it may well have been his influence that helped Master Nicholas to make his peace with authority in 1391.

While the evidence against individual knights is therefore slight and often ambiguous, the fact remains that the humbler Lollards persisted for years in the belief that they could look for help to the knightly class. Since they did so largely in vain, it must be presumed that they were mistaken. Thus, Swinderby's appeal to the commons to intercede for him was not effective. Yet it was long before his co-religionists abandoned hope of being able to induce parliament to set the church to rights. In 1395 when the estates were gathered in session a Lollard bill was affixed to the doors of Westminster Hall and St. Paul's.

'We poor men, treasurers of Christ and His apostles', ran its preamble, 'denounce to the lords and the commons of the parliament certain conclusions and truths for the reformation of holy church of England';

and twelve short paragraphs of contentious matter followed. There is no proof that it was taken notice of by parliament; and, apart from provoking a Dominican (who but for his cloth would have enjoyed the hereditary office of king's champion) to a lengthy rejoinder, it led to no action. The chronicler's tale that it obliged Richard II to cut short a visit to Ireland in order to hurry back to the church's defence is devoid of any truth.

All the same, even though the manifesto of 1395 failed in its immediate object, the ecclesiastical authorities were wise to take Lollard propaganda seriously. Their conviction that such holy mysteries as the heretics loved to discuss in the vulgar tongue were too deep for the laity's comprehension debarred them to some extent from answering it in kind. In any case, suppression as far as the uneducated people were concerned was safer than argument. The seizure and destruction of Lollard tracts, especially those written in English, and the punishment of anyone found owning or distributing them became a first object of official policy. When in the following century Reginald Peacock made the mistake of disputing with the 'lay party' in its own language he found himself, bishop though he was, condemned and imprisoned as a heretic. Theology was a subject for experts and could only be dealt with properly in Latin, a language which had two advantages over English: it was more precise and it was intelligible only to scholars.

In the early years of Wycliffe's attack upon the 'possessioners', when he still enjoyed considerable support even from churchmen, his victims had thought it imprudent to retort. But his doctrinal heresies made it safe for them to speak out and, as Courtenay's counter-attack was deployed, learned controversialists hastened to the task of examining, confuting and ridiculing Lollard error. The result was that just when the heretics were ceasing to be trained scholars, their master's works as well as their own more crudely-expressed theses became the objects of academic criticism. Wycliffe had left no disciple of like stature fit to defend his teaching in the schools. His opponents were legion; and not a few of them could match him single-handed. Among those who led a shattering onslaught on his opinions during the 1380s and 1390s, most of the religious orders were represented: the Benedictines Ughtred Boldon, Adam Easton and John Wells, the Cistercian William Remington, the Dominican Roger Dymoke, the Franciscan William Widford, the Austin Thomas Winterton, and Stephen Patrington and Thomas Netter, Carmelites. Many of their works survive unprinted and even unidentified along with those of their anonymous colleagues in our libraries. It is a great but common error to suppose that after Wycliffe the universities fell silent.

Though unable to answer the champions of orthodoxy on their own ground, the Lollards did not neglect to provide their followers with a literature suitable to their needs. Tracts and sermons in English, often translated or adapted from Wycliffe's Latin originals, were turned out in large numbers. But the most important undertaking of these years was a second translation of the Bible, a freer version than that originally put in hand by Nicholas Hereford. The completion of this laborious task can be assigned on the internal evidence of its general prologue to about the year 1396. The self-styled 'simple creature' who was responsible for it acknowledged the help of 'many good fellows and cunning at the translating'; but neither he nor they can be identified with any approach to certainty. The usual ascription to Purvey, though not unlikely, rests on slight foundation. To assume that he was the only Lollard in 1396 capable of doing the work, particularly when it was not a charge brought against him at his trial five years later, is to pile guesswork upon ignorance. But whoever the translator was he made a good job of it, and one entirely free from Lollard distortion. It is not surprising to learn that it was frequently found in the possession of those who repudiated the assumptions of the 'Bible men'. For this second unauthorised version had the merit of being intelligible as well as accurate.

The Lollard manifesto of 1395, despite its failure to win support in parliament, made a great stir among churchmen, since it seemed to prove that the measures so far taken to deal with heresy were quite inadequate. Since 1382 Courtenay and his suffragans had been vigilant and active; and 1388 had seen the beginnings of a more determined policy by the king's council for the suppression of heresy. Yet the number and insolence of their enemies, it could hardly be doubted, had steadily increased. The bishops felt that this was the right moment to appeal once again to the secular authorities for a more effective use of their coercive powers. In February 1395 the convocation of Canterbury passed the desired resolution and a copy of the 'Twelve Conclusions' of the Lollards was despatched to the pope to stir him into action.

Boniface IX, 'grieved from the bottom of [his] heart', thereupon wrote to King Richard on 17 September urging greater severity and diligence, so that 'there may not one spark remain hid under the ashes, but that it be utterly extinguished and speedily put out'. At the same time he sent letters to others, including the corporation of London, requesting them to put pressure on the government. Nothing having been done meanwhile, the prelates of both provinces seized the chance of a meeting of parliament in January 1397 to memorialise the king and lords. Hitherto the only public demand for the death penalty for heretics, of which there is evidence, had been that made by the friars of Leicester at Swinderby's trial before Buckingham in 1382. Now, fifteen years later, it was formally adopted by the rulers of the English church. They reminded parliament that when men were found guilty of the crime of heresy in other Christian realms they were straightway delivered over to secular judgement so that they might be put to death and their goods confiscated; and they begged for the aid of the lay arm against the malice of their foes. There is no record of any answer to this petition; certainly no statute was granted and no new vigilance is noticeable. But when Richard had been deposed and Henry of Lancaster had raised himself to the throne with the help of Courtenay's successor, Thomas Arundel, a fresh request was followed by legislation. By the statute of Heresy (*De Heretico Comburendo*) of 1401 an obstinate heretic or one who, having shown penitence, relapsed into error was upon conviction before an ecclesiastical court to be handed over to the sheriff to be burnt 'in a high place'. Thus England was brought by stages into conformity with the practice of western Christendom. The delay did not spring from a humane wish to avoid bloodshed, but from the novelty of the problem; the English had known little heresy before Wycliffe, but once they realised its dangers they did not shrink from employing the death penalty to stamp it out.

The first to be burnt at the stake was a priest from what was for Lollardy a new area: Norfolk. It was said of Henry Despenser, bishop of Norwich from 1370 to 1406, that he was a Lollard-hater and a Lollard-hunter, but he does not seem to have had much opportunity of indulging in the sport until 1399. On 30 April in that year a suspect was brought before him in his manor-house of South Elmham. This was William Sawtry, a man of unknown antecedents who was then employed as a chaplain in St.

Margaret's Lynn and at Tilney in the Norfolk fenland. Two days' examination produced a typical crop of false doctrines, revealing Sawtry as opposed to free will, image-worship and pilgrimage and decidedly shaky on the subject of the Eucharist. 'Mature deliberation'—in an episcopal prison, no doubt—convinced him of his errors, which he abjured at first privately and then on 25 May publicly in Lynn. Next day, in St. John's hospital there, before the bishop he swore on the Gospels never to preach the doctrines he had just renounced nor to hear confession without Despenser's licence.

It was therefore as a lapsed and contumacious heretic that he appeared before Archbishop Arundel on Saturday, 12 February 1401. To escape Despenser's attention he had removed himself from Norfolk to London where he got employment as the parish-priest of St. Osyth's, Walbrook. Here, it was said, he had taught and preached the like or similar heresies to those that he had before renounced. His guilt is hardly in doubt, but it is not easy to see anything very intelligible in his defence. Parliament had been sitting for more than a month when his trial began before a provincial council in the chapter-house of St. Paul's. It is therefore likely that the statute against heresy was already decided on, though it was not promulgated officially until the middle of March. This would explain the ironical and sometimes almost frivolous behaviour of the accused; he knew the strength of the case against him and he could foresee his end. If that is so, he did not altogether rise to the dramatic possibilities of his situation; the reports make him sound by turns obstinate, prevaricating, inconsistent and derisive. On 23 February he was publicly condemned and degraded from his orders by Arundel and six other bishops in St. Paul's. The archbishop took advantage of the ceremony to expound in English to the people the whole story of the trial. On the same day the king, with the backing of parliament, anticipated the statute and ordered the Londoners to commit Sawtry to the flames. Soon afterwards he was burnt to ashes at Smithfield, prophesying death and destruction for the king and kingdom. When his sins were committed, they had not been punishable with death; Sawtry did not face martyrdom from choice.

His fate was meant to act as a deterrent, and there can be little doubt that it worked successfully in the case of a much more distinguished Lollard than poor Sawtry. How and when John Purvey fell into the hands of his persecutors is not recorded. All we know is that on 28 February 1401 he was brought from the archbishop's prison in Saltwood castle, Kent, and accused before the provincial council still sitting in St. Paul's. Luckily for him, in all his twenty years' service as a Lollard teacher he had never been caught and therefore never forced to abjure. Notorious heretic though he was, he had no previous conviction. He could still save his skin—once—by admitting his fault and undergoing a humiliating public penance. Arundel was too busy to take part in his examination, which was committed to the bishops of Bangor and Rochester and occupied the best part of a week. It was the week in which Sawtry died. Purvey made his submission on 5 March and on the following day, Sunday, recanted the seven heresies proved against him at Paul's cross in the presence of the bishop of London, the earl of Warwick and many others. He could not complain that his sincerity was doubted; for in the following August he was inducted by the archbishop into the living of West Hythe, Kent. But he had been too long a hunted wanderer and a trusted leader to settle down comfortably in an isolated country vicarage. By October 1403 he had had enough, resigned his benefice and disappeared from sight. There is reason to believe that he was still alive in 1407, though no longer regarded by the authorities as dangerously heretical. The story that he underwent a further term of imprisonment is based on a confusion.

It was only to be expected that the Lollards would be mortified by his apostasy; he was one of the few surviving links with their founder. They were prepared to believe that he had succumbed to the rigours of his imprisonment at Saltwood, but even so they could not forgive his want of firmness. As one of them claims to have said to Arundel in 1407:

'Sir, Purvey is neither with you now for the benefice that ye gave him, nor holdeth he faithfully with the learning that he taught and writ before time; and thus he showeth himself neither hot nor cold.'

It was an ignominious end for Wycliffe's secretary, and protestants even now seem to find it hard to forgive him. But regrets that some Lollards 'lacked the spirit of martyrdom' (the phrase is Dr. Trevelyan's) come ill from those who have never been called upon to die for an unpopular opinion. Such hesitation should be easy to understand.

The first Englishman, if his own report be trusted, to defy the flames and to give Arundel as good as he got in argument was William Thorpe. Although he was not suspected until 1397, he claimed to be one of the generation of Wycliffe's Oxford followers and to have known Bishop Repton of Lincoln well in that prelate's unregenerate youth. About the master himself he spoke with devotion; 'and therefore of him specially and of these men I took my learning that I have taught; and purpose to live thereafter, if God will, to my life's end'. Of this thirty years as a preacher, the greater part was, it seems, spent in the north country. Arrested in 1397 but released without being compelled to make submission, he did not count as a lapsed heretic when he was once more in trouble ten years later. In 1406 he reproved Dr. Thomas Alkerton when the latter was preaching against a Lollard clerk of Oxford at Paul's cross; and meeting him that afternoon in Watling Street called him 'false flatterer and hypocrite!' But it was a sermon of his own at St. Chad's, Shrewsbury, on 17 March 1407, that so 'distroubled the commonalty' that the bailiffs of the town took him and handed him over to Arundel. In August he was brought to trial from confinement in Saltwood castle. His detailed record of the conversations he had with the archbishop naturally give him the better of the exchange, but also display his interrogator in quite a favourable light. He would have us believe that he stuck firmly to his creed, even when those about Arundel talked of burning him or throwing him into the sea. It is strange that there should be no official account of his examination and still more that there should be nothing to suggest that he met his death at the stake. On the other hand, his story is far too circumstantial to be plausibly dismissed as fiction. It leaves us the choice between doubting his fortitude or crediting Arundel with more compassion—and the power to exercise it—than he is usually allowed. At least Thorpe lived long enough to tell the tale.

Yet Arundel did on another occasion *show* mercy; that he did so in vain does not prove him a hypocrite. This was at the trial of John Badby, the tailor of Evesham who steadfastly refused to save his life by a recantation. Badby seems to have derived the extreme opinions he affected from some Bristol source. His denial of transubstantiation was vividly expressed: John Rakier of Bristol, he said, had as much power to make Christ's body as any priest. And when repeated admonitions had failed to subdue him or make him more respectful, he was pronounced an incorrigible heretic by Thomas Peverell, bishop of Worcester, in the charnel-chapel by the cathedral on 2 January 1409. After being kept for more than a year in prison he was brought before a crowd of bishops and lay lords presided over by Arundel in the Blackfriars at London on 1 March 1410. The record of the Worcester trial was read over in English and then the primate did his best to convince the Lollard 'in the bowels of Christ' that he was mistaken. But Badby could not be moved. He was given a few days to think matters over and then on 5 March he was again exposed to the arguments and prayers of the archbishops in St. Paul's, once more to no purpose. It only remained to confirm Peverell's verdict and to hand the prisoner over to the secular arm. Even so, Arundel urgently begged the temporal lords to spare Badby's life. We have no means of judging whether the plea was more than conventional, but it fell on deaf ears. Sentence had been passed in the morning; that afternoon it was carried out at Smithfield in the presence of many bishops and barons, including the king's eldest son. While the heretic was being fastened to the stake Prince Hal approached and tried to persuade him to recant; but Badby was unmoved.

His screams when the fire reached him were mistaken for repentance, so that the prince ordered the flames to be put out. Badby was lifted to the ground half-dead and while the clergy pressed round to receive his surrender, the prince, who 'thirsted sore for his salvation', offered him his life, liberty and a pension of threepence a day if he would conform. When he understood what was being said to him the scorched victim unflinchingly declined. He was tied afresh to the stake, the fire was rekindled and in a short while his sufferings reached an end. 'The wretch who mused further than his wit could stretch' could arouse even his executioners to pity by his courage at the stake. Yet less than a week later the statute of Heresy was read over in convocation as a warning to the indifferent; and when the commons in the parliament then sitting asked that one of its provisions might be modified the king rejected their petition.

This parliament of 1410 had already made itself offensive to orthodoxy by its willingness to entertain, if indeed not to inspire, a proposal for the disendowment of the possessioners. The confiscated temporalities were to be employed partly in relieving the King's treasury 'for defence of the realm' and partly to support a new nobility. After allowing Henry IV £20,000 a year, the sponsors reckoned that there would still be enough to endow fifteen new earls, 1,500 new knights and 6,200 new esquires. The arithmetic of the scheme was faulty, but it was unacceptable for other reasons. The King for one utterly repudiated its anti-clericalism; his trusted servant John Norbury delighted the monasteries by urging Arundel to crush these heretics; and the Prince of Wales was hostile. Even that part of the Lollards' programme most calculated to tempt the avarice of laymen could no longer be relied upon to earn them a hearing. The house of Lancaster was not receptive to those notions which had temporarily beguiled John of Gaunt.

As far as we know Sawtry and Badby were the only Lollards to suffer the extreme penalty in Henry IV's reign. The statute and the king's obvious determination to uproot heresy produced a bunch of edifying conversions and made the irreconcilables more cautious. But not all those in authority relished the duty of persecution; and many bishops took only the most perfunctory steps to hunt out and harry the secret congregations within their midst. Nor were the lay commissions appointed by the government any more active. It was not until the Lollard rising of 1414 that the number and distribution of those congregations stood revealed.

A minor revival of heresy at Oxford was, however, forced on the public notice by the injudicious zeal of some of its supporters. Courtenay's purge of the university was cleansing enough to last for a good many years after 1382. In July 1395 there seems to have been some anxiety in the king's council that all was not well and the university was instructed to drive out such as on examination were found to hold Lollard opinions. But it does not appear that anything came of it. Other evidence confirms the impression that a knowledge of Wycliffe's teaching survived in his university even though it did not attract much support. Thus the great Czech scholar and preacher, Jerome of Prague, who spent two years at Oxford round the turn of the century, was able to acquire and carry back to Bohemia several of Wycliffe's works. Others of his countrymen followed his example and within a few years copies of most of the English heretic's books were in the hands of the Czech reformers. It would not therefore be surprising if a few academic Lollards were found to have survived in circumspect obscurity at Oxford throughout these years. Unfortunately, nothing is known for certain until we come to Peter Payne.

Son of an English mother and a French father, Payne was born at Hough-on-the-Hill near Grantham about 1380. In 1406 he was already a graduate and had been introduced by a contemporary to Wycliffe's heresies. The contemporary, whose name was Partridge, had then taken fright and urged Payne to have nothing to do with doctrines that would prejudice his career. This worldly-wisdom was quickly rewarded as it deserved to be—with a benefice. But Payne was ardent, reckless and clever; and Wycliffe's heady wine had made him drunk. His first overt act was a piece of youthful folly: he wrote a letter in praise of the teacher whom he had never known, his spotless character, his truly Catholic fervour and his encyclopædic learning; and having by some subterfuge arranged to have the university seal attached to this effusive testimonial he sent it to the Prague reformers.

This escapade coming immediately after a Lollard sermon at Paul's cross by William Taylor, a clerk from Oxford, caused Archbishop Arundel to take quite disproportionate alarm. His fear that the university was once again becoming infested with heretics was based on ignorance. During the next few years it inspired a policy of censorship and repression that irritated many masters who had no truck with Lollardy. In November 1407 Arundel held a convocation at Oxford at which the new measures were promulgated. A committee of twelve was to examine the works of Wycliffe and to decide which might be used in the schools. And diligent enquiry was to be made into the orthodoxy of all resident scholars.

The university's dilatory execution of this repressive policy convinced Arundel that its sympathies were with the Lollards. It was, in fact, mainly concerned to preserve its academic liberties from outside interference. It had been trying for some years to secure exemption from archiepiscopal visitation and it was excusably offended by the primate's tactless and suspicious insistence on his rights. He had his way in the end. Two hundred and sixty-seven heretical or erroneous conclusions were detected in Wycliffe's writings; in July 1411, amid scenes of disorder, Arundel carried out his threatened visitation of the university, and by the close of the year he had extorted a full submission. Those who had resisted his progress were among the least heretical of Oxford's graduates. Protestants of a later age were deceived when they recognised them as Lollards. One of them, indeed, applied that name to the archbishop himself.

The Lollards were inevitably lost sight of amid the din of Arundel's quarrel with the privileged corporation. But surrender put an end to their immunity. Payne had meanwhile become principal of the academic hall dedicated to the memory of St. Edmund of Abingdon. He was now called upon as such to take an oath that he would not admit to the society under his charge 'any master, bachelor, scholar or servant who was in any way suspected of heretical pravity or Lollard opinion'. Other regulations made his own position increasingly perilous. Payne was a convinced Lollard and no dissembler, but he did not see any reason for becoming a martyr. When he was later taunted with cowardice he claimed that he refused to take the necessary oath and that the king supported him in his resistance. It is hard to follow this. The fact remains that he did not long continue at Oxford and that he fled the country before the end of 1413 to avoid a citation for heresy. He was to play an erratic but always honourable part in the religious struggles of the Czechs until his death forty years later.

The names of one or two of Payne's Oxford associates are known, but it is difficult to escape the impression that they were few. Only Ralph Mungin, who was his pupil in logic, is known as an active Lollard in later life; in 1428 he was condemned to perpetual imprisonment as a disseminator of heresy and heretical literature in London. Apart from this short-lived group at St. Edmund Hall, fifteenth-century Oxford seems to have been unexceptionably orthodox. Peter the Englishman was more at home in the university of Prague.

The Bohemian reformers lie outside the scope of this book, for the good reason that much as they studied Wycliffe's Latin writings and even borrowed heavily from them they were still not Wycliffites. Their origins, though in some respects similar, were independent and deep-rooted in their national history. By 1400 they were already too firmly committed to eucharistic orthodoxy for the Lollard attack on it to make any lasting impression on their thought. Their own leader and martyr, John Hus, was indebted to Wycliffe for his realist philosophy and for an example of defiance; but he could not accept the sacramental teaching of the Oxford doctor, still less the extreme iconoclasm of the latter's uneducated followers. Those who regard the Lollard denial of transubstantiation as growing inevitably out of Wycliffe's ultra-realism will find their refutation in the school of Prague. The Hussites saw no difficulty in stopping half-way along that route, in adopting the realism while discarding what are regarded as its logical consequences; that is to say, in occupying a position that for long satisfied Wycliffe himself. Their disagreements did not stand in the way of the growth of friendly relations between Bohemians and English. To each sect the other's existence was an encouragement. But the fact remains that there would still have been Hussites, and not very different ones at that, had there never been a Wycliffe. On the other hand, Hus, though he corresponded with the Lollards, had no discernible influence on their beliefs. In any case communication between the two bodies was short-lived; it seems to have come to an end with the disastrous failure of Oldcastle's rising in 1414.

Chapter Six

Oldcastle and Defeat

JOHN OLDCASTLE was born about 1378. His family, though of only moderate standing and wealth, had taken a worthy part in the local affairs of Herefordshire for at least two generations before he became its head. Both his grandfather and uncle had been knights of the shire in parliament and the latter had also been sheriff and escheator. Of the Lollard's early activities nothing is known, though he had succeeded to his inheritance, the manor of Almeley, before the end of the fourteenth century. His son and heir, another John, seems to have been born in 1396. He must therefore have married his first wife, Katherine daughter of Richard ap Jevan, before that date. She is known to have given him five children, two sons and three daughters, and to have died when she and her husband were still young. Like many other gentlemen of small fortune from Wales and its Marches, Sir John (he was already a knight in 1400) earned renown and a competence in the wars of the Lancastrian kings. He was on Henry IV's fruitless Scottish expedition of 1400 and saw considerable service thereafter against Owen Glendower and his Welsh. It was thus that he became the companion-in-arms and the personal intimate of the future Henry V, to whose household he became attached. In April 1406 the king rewarded his military exploits with an annuity for life of 100 marks. He had already found time to represent his native county in the parliament of January 1404, and in 1406–7 he served it as sheriff. By his thirtieth year he had won a name for himself as a tough fighter who enjoyed the confidence of the heir to the throne. It was then that a second marriage raised him to baronial rank.

His wife, Joan de la Pole, had already buried three husbands when in the summer of 1408 she ventured upon a fourth. She seems to have had a weakness for soldiers of fortune and, in all, married five of them. She was herself an heiress twice over—of her father, Sir John de la Pole, who died in 1380, and of her maternal grandfather John, lord Cobham, whose death in extreme old age occurred in January 1408. By marrying her, Oldcastle obtained the custody of a dozen scattered manors and of Cooling castle overlooking the Thames estuary. On the strength of this property and of his past services, he was in the following year summoned to parliament as a baron. He celebrated his good fortune by taking part in an Anglo-French tournament at Lille. So far no one had breathed a suspicion of his orthodoxy.

But practices that received small attention in remote Herefordshire could not safely be indulged in for long under the very nose of a wakeful archbishop. Arundel was at Dartford in the spring of 1410 when he learnt that one John, a chaplain dwelling under Oldcastle's roof, had been preaching heresy in the churches of Hoo, Halstow and Cooling, and particularly in the last, of which his host was patron. Too late to escape discovery, the rash offender had gone into hiding; only his baronial accomplice remained. Arundel's reception of this news makes it reasonably clear that he at once guessed Oldcastle's secret, but thought that it might still be possible to avert trouble. He cannot have known that he was dealing with a man who was unshakably committed to his heresies; for most men in Oldcastle's position a clear warning would have been enough. So on 3 April the archbishop ordered the prior of Rochester to put the three parishes under an interdict and to cite John the chaplain for trial. Then two days later 'out of reverence for' the lady Joan he relaxed the interdict and soon afterwards removed it altogether. But in future he had an eye on Cooling and its inhabitants.

How far Oldcastle was from heeding the primate's warning is shown by two letters which he caused to be written not long afterwards. The first, dated from Cooling castle on 8 September 1410, was addressed to a Bohemian noble who was a prominent supporter of Hus. Its purpose was to congratulate the Hussites on their recent successes and to exhort them to continue the struggle against the adherents of antichrist to the death. A year later Oldcastle wrote to King Wenceslas of Bohemia himself in similar terms, mentioning that he had also been in correspondence with Hus. The chief interest of these letters is their clear assumption that the writer was a recognised leader of the English sect; it is therefore probable that he had been an active heretic for some time. Yet, apart from the chaplain John, the only other Lollard with whom his association can be traced was a priest named Richard Wyche. From the diocese of Hereford Wyche had wandered preaching as far afield as Northumberland, where in 1400 he fell into the hands of Walter Skirlaw, bishop of Durham. It may have been a mere coincidence that Oldcastle was in that area in the same year. After prolonged examination and many attempts to persuade him to submit, Wyche was finally driven to recant by Purvey's example. He is next heard of writing to Hus from London on 8 September 1410. The letter had a similar purpose to that written by Oldcastle on the same day from Cooling: the noble congratulated the noble, the priest the priest; it is fairly obvious that they were accomplices.

In the autumn of 1411 Oldcastle was one of the captains sent by the prince of Wales to help the duke of Burgundy to recover Paris. If the prince still regarded him as a trustworthy subordinate, there cannot have been any widespread knowledge of his Lollard sympathies. Unlike some of his co-religionists, he was no pacifist. The expedition was a distinguished success. When, therefore, his friend succeeded Henry IV as king on 21 March 1413, Oldcastle could with justice look forward to high military employment in the new reign. But already in the convocation which began its debates on 6 March, damning evidence against him was being brought to light. It remained to be seen whether Henry V would allow him to be persecuted.

In St. Paul's on the first day of convocation Arundel's registrar had just examined the credentials of those answering the primate's summons when he was informed that there was present in the church a chaplain who was highly suspect as a heretic, accompanied by two other unknown men. The registrar immediately sent for the chaplain and cross-examined him. His name, the man replied, was John Lay; he was attached to St. Mary's church, Nottingham, and came from those parts; he had arrived in London two days before and that very morning had celebrated mass in Sir John Oldcastle's presence. But when he was asked for his credentials and his bishop's licence, Lay answered that he had failed to bring them with him. He was given a week to produce them. The episode has many odd features and suggests that Oldcastle was being watched. Unfortunately, there is no record of any sequel. One is left to assume that Lay, like John the chaplain, who may, indeed, have been the same man, made himself scarce.

Convocation, one gathers, then turned to other questions, but it can hardly have come as a surprise to anybody when the search of an illuminator's shop in Paternoster Row led to the discovery of a number of heretical tracts belonging to Oldcastle. This was evidence that he would find it difficult to explain away and it was decided at once to inform the king. A meeting took place in the inner chamber of the royal manor of Kennington at which both Henry V and Oldcastle were present. Some of the most heretical passages in the confiscated literature were read aloud and greatly shocked the king; never, he said, had he heard worse matter. Turning to Oldcastle, he challenged him to disagree. Oldcastle was unruffled, answering that the doctrines recited deserved condemnation, and excused his possession of the tracts on the ground that he had only dipped into them without grasping their character. If this satisfied the king, it quite failed to impress the clergy, who withdrew to prepare a more extensive indictment of the accused.

This, at any rate in the summarised form which has come down to us, was full of generalities and devoid of factual detail. Oldcastle was alleged to have uttered and maintained heretical doctrines in many places, to have given aid and comfort to Lollard preachers and to have terrorised those opposed to them. In short he 'was and is the principal harbourer, promoter, protector and defender' of heretics, especially in the dioceses of London, Rochester and Hereford. When the lower clergy pressed for his trial and condemnation the prelates pointed out that more circumspect treatment was desirable in the case of one who was a member of the king's domestic circle. It was therefore agreed that Henry should once more be consulted. A second visit to Kennington found him sympathetic towards the church's case, but anxious to do all he could to avoid the public humiliation of a trusted servant. He asked the clergy to wait while he tried the effect of a personal appeal; should he fail to move Oldcastle, then he promised to throw the full weight of the secular arm on to the side of the church. This was reluctantly agreed to.

Henry's hopes of an obliging submission were disappointed. Oldcastle was obdurate and in August the king wrote to tell Arundel to proceed in accordance with the law. But when the primate tried to serve the accused with a formal summons the gates of Cooling castle were shut against his officer. This defiance was as short-lived as it was foolish and by 23 September Oldcastle, who had meanwhile sought another interview with the king at Windsor and been arrested for his pains, was a prisoner in the Tower of London. On that day his trial opened before Arundel, assisted by the bishops of London and Winchester in St. Paul's. He was at once promised full forgiveness in return for submission. But deprived though he was of the king's protection, Oldcastle was unwilling to admit his guilt. Instead, he treated his ecclesiastical judges to a statement of his views which lacked precision on all the material points. Arundel was not convinced; he had had to do with such documents before. He admitted that as far as it went the confession of faith was satisfactory but he would like plain answers to two plain questions: Did Sir John believe in transubstantiation and did he regard confession to a priest as necessary in the sacrament of penance? Oldcastle at first refused to say another word. Then, irritated by the steady pressure to which he was submitted, he denied the right of popes, cardinals and bishops to lay down what should be believed about such matters. Even so, Arundel's scrupulousness was inexhaustible. He gave the prisoner a week-end to think over his plight and provided him with a statement in English of the orthodox doctrine on the disputed points. He had little hope of securing a conversion or he would not have reinforced the court so powerfully for its next session.

He again began the proceedings on Monday, 25 September, with a conditional offer of absolution. Oldcastle first declined to be absolved by anyone other than God. Then he went on to assert that the bread remained bread after consecration and that confession, though sometimes expedient, was never essential to salvation. Next he broke into a tirade against the hierarchy: the pope was the head of antichrist, the bishops his members and the friars his tail. And, finally, raising his hands he warned the crowd of spectators that those who judged and wished to condemn him were deceivers and would lead them to hell. It is recorded that the archbishop once more implored him in tears to return to the bosom of the church. Then, seeing that it was vain to wrestle with him any longer, he delivered the judgement of the court. Oldcastle was excommunicated and left to the mercy of the secular arm.

For this trial we are wholly dependent upon the formal report prepared by Arundel's registrar and circulated throughout the province of Canterbury. It is impossible to say how far the primate's care to give the accused every possible chance should be accepted as genuine. On the other hand, those who doubt it have nothing but a disposition to believe the worst of ecclesiastical judges to justify their scepticism. Again and again the official records emphasise Arundel's patience, fairness and anxiety to avoid the extreme penalty if he possibly could. I am inclined to believe that the impression these documents convey is an accurate one. Oldcastle had had every chance, but he was a conscientious Lollard and when offered a choice between recantation or death he was too straightforward and too brave to deny his faith. There is no need to take sides. It is difficult to see how either man believing what he did could have acted differently.

The king shared the primate's scruples. He, too, could not give up hope of a last-minute change of heart. So instead of ordering an immediate execution (as was usual) he allowed Oldcastle a respite of forty days, to be spent as a prisoner in the Tower. This interval had more than half elapsed without the desired result when, on the night of 19 October, the condemned man succeeded in making his escape from the fortress with the help of some London friends. He did not attempt to leave the capital but lay in hiding under the roof of one of his rescuers, a Lollard bookseller called William Fisher, near St. Sepulchre's, Smithfield, while he was searched for in vain. The next weeks were spent in planning revenge and an end of persecution. A wild attempt was to be made to capture the king and to seize political power by force of arms. The story of this abortive rising, which displayed the weakness and ineptitude of the English heretics, has never been adequately told. Yet it offers us our one serious chance of measuring the achievement of the Lollard missionaries and of estimating whether the secret followers of Wycliffe were numerous and powerful enough (as those in authority feared) to threaten the stability of church and kingdom. For no other incident in the history of the sect are the materials as plentiful or as informative.

The fact of Oldcastle's escape seems at first to have been hushed up. Even the king may not have been told until 28 October, when he removed the keeper of the Tower and sent him to prison for his negligence. On the same day his subjects were forbidden by proclamation to succour the fugitive. November and December then passed without any overt sign of what was afoot, but the government was on the alert, having reason to suspect the existence of treasonable designs among the nobility quite unconnected with Oldcastle's plot. As a result, it got wind of the Lollards' intention just in time to take measures to thwart it. After the rising had failed, Thomas Burton, 'the king's spy', was given £5 as a reward for 'his assiduous watchfulness' in reporting the plans of the traitors to his master. Two other men received pensions for detecting and revealing the existence of the conspiracy. But when Henry set out to pass Christmas with his brothers and a number of other lords at the royal manor of Eltham in Kent, he did not yet know that he was in any danger.

The New Year found the court still in residence at Eltham and intending to celebrate the feast of the Epiphany (6 January) there also. Meanwhile, in various parts of the country Lollard agents, instructed by Oldcastle, were busy rousing the members of their sect. The well-disposed were begged to take up arms and march to his aid; the less well-disposed were offered money for their services. Small parties were to converge on London, choosing as their *rendezvous* the fields outside the walls of the city to the north-west of Temple Bar. Here their leader would meet them on the night of 9–10 January and with their help secure quick possession of the capital. While this was being accomplished a picked band of conspirators, disguised as mummers, were to present themselves before the court at Eltham and there 'under cover of the mumming' capture the entire royal family.

It was a reckless enterprise, the scheme of an injured and desperate man. The numbers required for its execution could hardly have been collected without attracting notice; and not all Lollards could be relied upon to turn traitors for the sake of their creed. At the last moment some of those involved betrayed the details of their plot to the king, who at once notified the magistrates of the city. The result was that at ten o'clock in the evening of Twelfth Night the mayor went 'with a strong power' to the sign of the Axe without Bishopsgate, the place of business of John Burgate, a Lollard carpenter. Here he surprised and arrested Burgate and seven other would-be mummers, including one of Oldcastle's esquires, before they had received their cue. Taken to Eltham, they were examined before the king and induced to confess. Another Lollard haunt, perhaps that of Oldcastle himself, the Wrestler-on-the-Hoop in Smithfield, was overlooked. In spite of this set-back the conspiracy was not called off. With many of his provincial followers already up in arms, its leader had good reason for feeling that it was too late to draw back. Yet without the advantage of surprise it was hardly possible to win.

Twelfth Night that year fell on a Saturday. The occasion selected by Oldcastle for his attempted *coup d'état* was the dawn of the Wednesday following. On the Monday, King Henry and his three brothers, instead of remaining at Eltham as they had proposed, still further upset their enemy's calculation by transferring themselves to Westminster. They were protected by a numerous retinue, and several earls and bishops were in attendance. The Lollards of the capital, on whom much depended, may well have been thrown into confusion by the arrest of Burgate and his friends and by the other royal countermeasures. At any rate, when the decisive moment arrived few or none of them turned out. Their desertion, we are told, 'wonderfully discouraged' those captains of the heretics who had optimistically looked for the help of thousands.

Unaware of the Londoners' discomfiture, their provincial allies, some of whom had been more than a week *en route*, walked blindly into the king's trap. Those from the midland shires passed near to the Hertfordshire abbey of St. Albans and moved old Thomas Walsingham in his study there to a characteristic description. 'You might see the crowds,' he wrote.

'drawn by large promises from almost every county in the realm, hastening along by footpaths, high roads and byways to meet at the day and hour then at hand. When asked why they hurried thus and ran themselves nearly out of breath, they answered that they were going as fast as they could to join their lord Cobham who had paid them a retaining fee and was now in need of their service.'

No attempt was made to stop these rustic simpletons before they reached their destination. Their numbers, as the records show, were wildly exaggerated by the chronicler.

The king was ready for them. Though some of his advisers favoured caution, he was resolved to scatter the bands of insurgents before the light of dawn permitted them to join forces. The gates of the city were guarded to prevent them from making contact with their friends within; the sanctuary at Westminster was searched by the duke of Clarence in case Oldcastle lay hidden there to threaten the king's rear; careful watch was kept everywhere; and troops were drawn up across the principal approaches to the rebels' meeting-place in St. Giles's Fields. Soon after midnight Henry took his place in command of the main army covering the road to Westminster. Since darkness concealed the details of what followed, it is not surprising that the accounts are confused and vague. There was very little fighting. When they blundered unexpectedly upon the royal troops in the night most of the countrymen lost their nerve and turned tail. Although they were hotly pursued, some did manage to make good their escape. A few who tried to resist capture were struck down. Quite a number—'eighty or more', according to a London source—were taken prisoner; among them were some of the ringleaders, but Sir John Oldcastle again succeeded in eluding his enemies. Dawn found Henry in possession of the field after a rout that is not known to have cost him a single casualty.

Decisive the victory may have been, but it could not be regarded as particularly glorious. With very few exceptions, the Lollards were no match for Henry's trained knights and men-at-arms. Their 'armies' were composed of chaplains, weavers, shoemakers, glovers, tailors, goldsmiths, carpenters and ploughmen. Of those whose occupations were recorded, most were weavers. Regarded as fighting soldiers, these craftsmen were scarcely better than Falstaff's rogues in buckram. It is unlikely that many of them had had much experience of war or were even adequately armed. The case of their leaders was naturally different. Oldcastle was a hardened veteran and was able to draw a few others of like background into the adventure. There was, for example, his personal esquire, John Brown; above all, there was Sir Roger Acton of Sutton near Tenbury in Worcestershire, whom men regarded as his principal lieutenant. A tiler's son from

Shrewsbury, Acton had, like his commander, done well enough out of Henry IV's wars to be able to set up as a landowner. His association with a Lollard chaplain was scarcely close enough to justify the belief that he shared Oldcastle's religious tastes. Another campaigner in the Welsh Marches, Sir Thomas Talbot of Davington, near Faversham in Kent, was also involved in the rising; as were Robert Harley and Richard Colfox 'of London', esquires of doubtful antecedents, and Thomas Noveray, 'gentleman', of Illston-on-the-Hill in Leicestershire. Suspicion also for a time rested on a number of other members of the landed class, not, it seems, without reason; but if they were aware of what was being planned and even hoped to reap benefit from its success, they were wise enough to take no active part. Doubtless, those of the gentry who did, could have given a good account of themselves had the odds against them been less heavy. Once the advantage of surprise had passed from them to the king, the issue was not in doubt.

Had they succeeded in both their immediate objectives —to kidnap the royal brothers and to occupy London before the alarm was raised—the rebels would still have been far short of complete victory. They would, however, have held a strong position from which to bargain. What they ultimately hoped to achieve is far from clear; indeed, it may never have been precisely formulated. In official proclamations they were credited with the intention of wiping out the royal family, the nobility and the higher clergy, of stripping the church of its great possessions and of dividing the kingdom up among themselves under the regency of Oldcastle. Improbable though this sounds, it is difficult to see how they could safely have done less. One of their number, a rich brewer of Dunstable called Robert Morley, was rumoured to have been promised all Hertfordshire for his share. Of a hopeful disposition, he brought two horses with gold trappings and a pair of gilt spurs with him in readiness for his promotion. This Sancho Panza was caught in the bishop of London's park at Harringay and lodged in the Tower. It is a matter for regret that he and his like were not given a chance to show what they meant to do. It could hardly have been greater folly than their conqueror's first invasion of France.

No time was wasted by the government in taking measures to restore order, to bring the prisoners to a speedy trial and to round up the majority who were still at large. On 10 January, a few hours after the victory of St. Giles's Fields, a commission was appointed to enquire concerning all treasons, insurrections and felonies committed in London and Middlesex and to deal with those found guilty in accordance with the law. The commissioners set to work at once in summary fashion. By Friday, the 12th, sixty-nine of their prisoners had been condemned to death. An ecclesiastical court took even less time to investigate the state of their souls. Next day thirty-eight of them were drawn on hurdles from Newgate to the scene of their intended triumph in St. Giles's Fields, where four pairs of new gallows had been erected for the occasion. There they were hanged side by side in batches. The bodies of seven who had been found guilty of obstinate heresy as well as treason were afterwards burnt. Those despatched for execution were headed by Robert Harley and included two clerks in holy orders. A week later four more victims suffered a like fate.

Meanwhile, care was being taken of the fugitives and the stay-at-home sympathisers. On 11 January the king appointed commissioners in London, Bristol and twenty shires whose task it was to draw up lists of suspects and to collect sworn evidence against them. Anyone who came under their unfavourable notice was to be arrested and gaoled until the king and council had decided what to do with him. Soon afterwards the business of trying prisoners was committed to the justices of King's Bench. The investigation thus ordered did not take long in getting under way. We owe to the commissioners' findings most of our knowledge of the rising, of the men taking part in it and of their geographical distribution. As a result, a good many rebels, as well as a number of notorious Lollards who were presumed to be accessories, were identified and brought into court. Towards the end of January John Brown, Oldcastle's esquire, was caught in

Oxfordshire—through which he was probably making his way to the Welsh border—and taken to London for trial and execution. Finally, the royal officers succeeded in arresting Sir Roger Acton; he faced his judges at Westminster on 8 February and two days later, after a jury had found him guilty, was hanged in St. Giles's Fields.

By the end of March the king had decided upon clemency, at least for the deluded rank and file. On the 28th of that month all except a dozen named traitors and those either in custody or released on bail were offered charters of pardon provided that they came and sued for them before midsummer. Those who had been convicted and were in prison awaiting execution were allowed to cool their heads for a year or so and then released. Since the king's pardon did not cover any breach of the church's law, many were handed over to their bishops for ghostly correction before they received their freedom. Lest any traitor should survive to cause future disturbance, parliament in the spring of 1414, meeting at Leicester, the heretics' metropolis, placed the responsibility for hunting out and destroying Lollardy upon the shoulders of every royal and municipal officer.

Presentments made to the king's commissioners by local juries in the weeks following the rising provide evidence of the extent to which Oldcastle's agents had succeeded in their task. As was to be expected, the areas that had responded with most alacrity to their call were roughly those in which Lollardy had for many years been troublesome. To this general rule some interesting exceptions should be noted. Distance rather than lack of sympathy may account for the failure of the border-lands of Shropshire and Herefordshire to produce contingents. But it cannot explain why Oldcastle's Kentish tenants and neighbours remained obstinately aloof; the sermons of John the chaplain in the hundred of Hoo cannot have done as much harm as Arundel feared. Apart from Sir Thomas Talbot, who was in any case a newcomer to the district, the only known rebel of Kentish origin was a townsman of Dover. East Anglia appeared no more enthusiastic; a single native of the diocese of Norwich,

Edmund Frith of Mildenhall, was reported an object of suspicion. Since it was not many years before this area had its flourishing Lollard congregations, its failure to participate in the rising seems to emphasise its remoteness from the rest of England.

In marked contrast with the inertness of the East Anglians was the lively response of the men of Essex, among whom Lollardy had not previously been in evidence. The findings of the local juries suggest that the main responsibility lay with one William, the parish priest of Thaxted, who since Michaelmas 1402 had been wandering unmolested about the northern parts of the county as far afield as Maldon, preaching heresy. In his own village he had the help of John Smith, a shoemaker, who possessed English books and taught opinions contrary to the Catholic faith to its inhabitants. The other places affected —Coggeshall, Pattiswick, Kelvedon, Halstead and Colchester—were all within William of Thaxted's range. The town of Colchester was reported to boast a little group of Lollard students who, with the support of a Franciscan called John Brettenham, met together in their homes to read devotional literature, but these left active participation in the revolt to others. The most determined adherents of Oldcastle in north Essex were the brothers John and Thomas Cook, weavers of Pattiswick. On 1 January John promised some craftsmen of the nearby village of Kelvedon 6d. a day each to rise against the king; accordingly, on the 6th two set off in arms for St. Giles's Fields. The evidence suggests that the Essex contingent was one of those to resist capture and to suffer therefore fairly heavy casualties, including the Cook brothers, when they came into contact with the king's men.

In Leicestershire, where heresy was still widely prevalent, the copying and distribution of Oldcastle's broadsheets was undertaken by Thomas Ile, from the well-established Lollard centre outside the county at Braybrooke. He gave one, it was said, to William Smith of Leicester, perhaps the same man who had submitted to Courtenay in 1389. More certainly a hardened sinner was John Belgrave, also of Leicester. There had been complaints against him some years before because he had likened an ecclesiastical judge to those who had condemned Susannah. No one could therefore be surprised to hear him in 1414 slandering the pope and the bishops and declaring that the papacy had been vacant since the first century. Another outstanding anti-clerical speaker, Ralph Friday, of the same town, was reported to have described Arundel as a disciple of antichrist. The first breach of the peace occurred on 26 December at Belton in Charnwood, where two men, Ward, a ploughman, and another William Smith, armed themselves and took horse for London. They were joined on 5 January by a handful of Lollards from Mountsorrel, Sileby and Leicester itself. Meanwhile, on the previous day, at Kibworth Harcourt to the south-east, about a dozen peasants from it and the surounding villages—Smeeton Westerby, Shangton, Saddington and Kibworth Beauchamp—had declared for Oldcastle. The ringleader thereabouts was Walter Gilbert, a chaplain who was said to have induced two labourers to join him by bribing them with twenty shillings; he and his kinsman, Nicholas Gilbert, were among those hanged a week later in St. Giles's Fields. It is tempting to attribute the existence of Lollardy in this corner of Leicestershire to William Swinderby's sermons at Market Harborough. But Sir Thomas Latimer had been lord of Smeeton Westerby, and another and more recent influence was Thomas Noveray of Leicester, whose home was close by at Illston. On the same day as the Kibworth rising took place, Noveray left Illston to join Oldcastle.

Walter Gilbert had not confined his activities to his native village. Under the name of Walter Kibworth, he was as well known in Derby and its environs, where, after the rising had been suppressed, Henry Booth, an esquire of Littleover, was charged with having sheltered him, knowing him to be a Lollard. Three of those executed on 13 January were tradesmen of Derby; a weaver of Chaddesden was condemned to death but later reprieved. At Thulston, five miles out of Derby on the London road, another agitator had been at work. This was a chaplain named William Ederick, who since 1410 had been assiduously spreading error in Derby, Tutbury and elsewhere from a base at Aston-upon-Trent. Here he was housed and maintained by Thomas Tickhill, a successful lawyer, and his wife Agnes. On 30 December 1413 Ederick managed to persuade four men of Thulston, a smith, a weaver, a thatcher and a mason, to take a wage of 13s. 4d. for escorting him in arms to the insurgents' camp. The Tickhills wisely remained at home, but their offence of harbouring a notorious Lollard afterwards cost the husband some months' imprisonment in the Tower.

Elsewhere in the midlands the same kind of thing happened. From Warwickshire only the men of Coventry seem to have been drawn in; their leader was Ralph Garton, a mercer of the town, but they were neither many nor prominent at St. Giles's Fields. A score or so of rebels from Northampton, Daventry and the places round about them were delated to the king's commissioners. Robert Morley of Dunstable seems to have had few adherents in Bedfordshire, and Hertfordshire is only known to have contributed two villagers from Bovingdon, both executed, two from Great Gaddesden and one from Hitchin. Outside London the only other districts that sent more than an isolated volunteer to Oldcastle's standard were the Chilterns, the lower valley of the river Cherwell and the great port of Bristol.

Lollardy among the Buckinghamshire hills seems to have owed much to the ancient family of Cheyne of Drayton Beauchamp, several members of which had earlier come under suspicion. In 1414 its head had bestowed the livings of Drayton itself and Chenies upon heretics. Three Cheynes were implicated in the rising; one of them very probably lost his life in it. Other centres were Amersham and Little Missenden, both of which had their martyrs on the gallows in St. Giles's; and Wycombe, having sent a number of its sons, was lucky to avoid a like distinction. Nonconformity persisted in this area throughout the fifteenth century.

William Brown, *alias* Davy, a glover of Woodstock, was the moving spirit among the Oxfordshire Lollards. He drew his followers from several nearby villages: Bladon,

Handborough, Kidlington, Kirtlington and Upper Hey-
ford. Two members of the university were involved, one
the principal of Cuthbert Hall, but the contingent that
set off for London on 2 January was far from academic;
it included a fuller, a tailor, a cooper, a carpenter, a
miller and a mason. Behind them came Sir Roger Acton,
who, leaving his home at Sutton on the 6th, was joined
by a goldsmith at Worcester and passed through Evesham
on the Wycombe–London road the following day. Finally,
the largest single party of rebels was that which rode out
of Bristol on Thursday, 4 January, allowing itself five days
to cover rather less than 120 miles. Composed of some
forty craftsmen, for the most part weavers, it was headed
by as many as six chaplains, the chief of whom was known
both as Walter Blake and as Walter More. They were
said to have laid out a large sum of money on bows and
arrows and other gear for Oldcastle's army. Their leader
and three or four of his followers paid for their faith with
their lives.

This rapid survey of a considerable mass of evidence
will enable some deductions to be drawn. In the first
place it is clear that the response to Oldcastle's appeal was
miserably small. Doubtless not all those participating who
managed to get away were denounced by their more loyal
neighbours, but the fewness of the prisoners taken em-
phasises the minute scale of the affair. Far from there
being, as both chroniclers and indictments alleged, twenty
or even twenty-five thousand Lollards in arms, it does not
seem likely that there were half as many hundreds, or,
indeed, anything like it. If a list is made of all who are
known to have been wanted, arrested, tried, executed or
pardoned by the authorities, it adds up to only two or
three hundred. Yet there is no reason to think that the
royal officials were either ill-informed or lax in their
efforts to round up every traitor; while, to judge from the
evidence of the presentments, the country had been
genuinely shocked by the attempt on the king's life and
was anxious to bring the guilty to justice.

Secondly, the records make it difficult to believe that
anything like all taking part were convinced Lollards

whose actions were dictated by the faith they shared. The proportion of those both hanged and burnt on 13 January to those only hanged, namely 7 to 31, is surely evidence of that. There was little to be gained by a last-minute recantation; death faced them in either case. Yet less than a fifth were judged worthy of the fire. Again, only some of those pardoned were handed over to their ecclesiastical superiors when the king ordered their release from his prisons. In this connection it is as well to remember how some of the rebels had been attracted by offers of pay. It would not be surprising if such offers recruited the gullible, the needy, the foolhardy and the criminal to the cause. Nor were only the humble exposed to such temptations. Robert Morley of Dunstable may have been a genuine heretic, but he had another inducement: the promise of Hertfordshire. Even so prominent a traitor as Sir Roger Acton, notwithstanding the rumour that he had a Lollard chaplain, was only hanged; for we are specifically told that his body was cut down and given burial after a month. That he and other military free-lances joined Oldcastle is less evidence of religious conviction than of a desire for a gambler's reward. There is nothing to suggest that such a man as Sir Thomas Beauchamp of White Lackington, Somerset, who spent eight months in the Tower in 1414, was anything but orthodox. The lenient view that Henry took of his and others' complicity in the plot seems to recognise that they were mere adventurers without principle.

The part played by the heretic clergy as the recruiting-sergeants of the movement is hardly surprising. More noteworthy is the extent to which the existence of Lollard communities willing to respond to propaganda depended upon the active preaching and instruction of a few devoted priests. Bristol's complement of six chaplains had no parallel; elsewhere the task fell as a rule to a single minister, aided perhaps by one or two enthusiastic lay readers. In some towns, such as Leicester and Northampton, the hold of the new doctrines over the class of small artisans and tradespeople was lasting and, it seems, deep. In the countryside, on the other hand, nonconformity to survive needed to be tended and renewed. Even here it was most tenacious in places that boasted a cottage industry or two, like glove-making at Woodstock and weaving in many districts. But much turned on the zeal and skill of the individual missionary. It is evident that heresy in Essex owed everything to the preaching tours of William the chaplain of Thaxted. Walter Gilbert and William Ederick were likewise responsible for spreading the word among the rural population of the northern midlands. They in their turn, as the documents show, depended upon the material help and protection of the landed gentry. It has been seen how Braybrooke and Chipping Warden became Lollard centres, thanks to Sir Thomas Latimer. The patronage of Thomas Compworth in the lower valley of the Cherwell and that of the Cheynes in Buckinghamshire were hardly less fruitful. Even so, the impression derived from the records is that everywhere, in town and country alike, the heretics formed an insignificant minority.

Not that they were confined to the hot-heads who took part in Oldcastle's rash attempt. In addition to presenting those who were actually in arms or were accessories before the fact, the juries, as they were required to do, named a good many less guilty offenders. These included those commonly defamed as Lollards, those who were known to have harboured unlicensed preachers, who possessed heretical or merely English devotional books or were in the habit of attending conventicles to hear false doctrine propounded. Some preachers of the word, wholly innocent of treasonable knowledge, were consequently apprehended. They rarely came to worse harm at the king's hands than a short spell of imprisonment; but they may have had more trouble in escaping the attention of their bishops. Unfortunately, no episcopal register contains any evidence of the proceedings that must have been taken against them. A group of suspected Bristol laymen, who appeared before Bishop Bubwith of Wells in July 1414, were kept in prison for six months and even after that not wholly freed from observation. The clergy are hardly likely to have been accorded a more favourable reception.

It is wellnigh impossible to calculate the number of those with Lollard sympathies too timid, too pacific or too law-abiding to declare themselves while the issue was in doubt, who also succeeded in escaping notice in the subsequent enquiry. One cannot be sure that Oldcastle commanded the allegiance of the whole sect. Was it indeed a *sect*, an organised church with some kind of central direction and a common creed? Very little light on this problem can be derived from the sources. Walsingham, it is true, informs us that by 1389 the Lollards had usurped the bishop's right of ordination; they were making priests in the diocese of Salisbury. But this does not seem to have been more than a haphazard attempt to supply a local need. There is no evidence that illicit ordination was commonly resorted to. Like the early methodists, the Lollards did not wish to secede from the church; they wished to restore it to its antique pattern. It is unlikely, therefore, that they formed a society with terms of admission, the right to discipline its members and if necessary the power to expel them. On the other hand, one gets the impression that the various congregations were loosely affiliated and that the doctrines taught in them were nowhere widely different. Though the evidence for a central committee is virtually lacking, the fact that Oldcastle was able to summon help from a dozen shires does make some rudimentary form of organisation at least probable.

Nevertheless, that does not mean that every Lollard responded; nor is it likely that all were reached in the time available. Men who are known to have been heretics both before and after 1414—William Taylor, for example, or Richard Wyche—were in no way implicated in the rising nor discovered in the investigation which resulted from it. They lay low or were protected by friendly jurors. It is noteworthy how many of the places connected with Lollardy were on the chief highways of medieval England. These were naturally most accessible to Oldcastle's agents, as they were to the commissions of enquiry. But for the same reason they were most exposed to infection by itinerant preachers and it may well be that Lollard traffic was restricted almost entirely to the main roads. Even so, the government's failure to track down some of those who escaped warns us not to over-estimate the efficiency of its agents. All that can be safely deduced is that the isolated and obscure colonies of heretics that evaded notice were neither as many nor as large as those subjected to official visitation and correction. The alarmist fears of those in authority that English society was so riddled with heresy that the realm no less than the church was in danger were wildly exaggerated. To the lawlessness from which medieval England was a chronic sufferer, the new sect's contribution was far from large.

Finally, no student can fail to notice how tenuous had become the connection of Lollardy with Oxford. Only a tiny fraction of the clergy involved were graduates; most of them seem to have been unbeneficed chaplains; the principal of Cuthbert Hall, John Mybbe, was the only resident master to come under suspicion. When it is remembered what sort of people were Lollards, this is not surprising. Only the few gentry who dabbled in heresy had livings to bestow; the rest were inevitably content with the ministrations of those drawn from their own class. The prevalence of Lollardy among the new industrial groups both in town and village is one of the most obvious lessons of the revolt. Particularly noticeable is the number who were concerned with the processing of cloth, were fullers, dyers, weavers, tailors. The presence of a few scriveners and parchment-makers hardly supports the view that the book-trade was a channel of Lollard propaganda. But it is clear that in those crafts where literacy was usual or necessary the tendency towards heresy was strongest. Ecclesiastics who mistrusted a reading layman and regarded the possession of vernacular literature as evidence of depravity were not entirely wrong. A good many of those accused of being eloquent and forceful preachers of the word were not in orders.

Heading the list of traitors for whom on 28 March 1414 no pardon was forthcoming was inevitably the name of Sir John Oldcastle. Large rewards had been offered for his capture since the morrow of the rebellion, but, nevertheless, his hiding-place was not revealed. Too late the royal officers searched the house in which he had been concealed until 9 January. After being formally summoned the required number of times to come to the shire court of Middlesex, he was outlawed at Brentford on 14 June 1414. Then calculation inclined the king to mercy. Henry was preparing to invade France; the need to secure peace in England during his absence made him willing to pardon even Oldcastle, but only if he came out of hiding and surrendered himself. This concession was proclaimed on 9 December; when by 18 February 1415 it had failed of its purpose, it was repeated with still greater urgency. Henry was obliged to set sail in August without the satisfaction of knowing that the leader of the heretics was under surveillance. Rumours were rife at this time about the Lollards' intention to revenge their defeat, but they were not too well-founded. Walsingham tells us that Oldcastle was nearly caught near Malvern on the eve of the king's departure. On 14 August he is known to have been entertained at Chesterton in Warwickshire by its former vicar, John Prest. Then for two years all track of him was lost. A criminal tried to save his skin by concocting an incredible tale about meeting the fugitive at the prior of Wenlock's table in April 1417 and being asked to mint base coin on his behalf; but, although he succeeded in getting the prior, John Mar, arrested, the latter was able to persuade the court of his innocence. A little later Oldcastle was reported in the neighbourhood of St. Albans in the house of one of the abbot's serfs; a raid on the suspected place of concealment drew blank, though the monks, at least, persuaded themselves that traces of his presence were discovered.

At length his pursuers picked up a genuine scent. On 15 July 1417, accompanied by a London mercer, he spent some time at Byfield in Northamptonshire. Two husbandmen and their wives who received, comforted and sustained the wanted men were afterwards put on trial. Next, five weeks later, on 20 August, Oldcastle had reached his old home at Almeley, where he tried to persuade or coerce some of his former tenants into providing him with food and service. By the time this affair was investigated in January 1418, the chase was over. Some time in the autumn of 1417 Oldcastle's presence in the neighbourhood of Welshpool became known to Sir Griffith Vaughan, a local land-owner. Vaughan sent two of his sons to take the outlaw. They were not successful without a fight, in which their prey was wounded—it is said that he was not overpowered until a woman struck him on the shin with a stool—so that he had to be conveyed to Westminster in a horse-drawn litter, known as a 'whirlicote'. On 14 December he was led before parliament. He had already been condemned as a traitor and excommunicated as an incorrigible heretic. Nothing remained to be done, but he was given a chance to speak in mitigation of his crimes. The words put into his mouth by the St. Albans writer have suggested to some that his mind had been affected by his ill-treatment. But since the official record says that he made no reply, this deduction seems unnecessary. On the same day he was removed to the Tower, drawn through the city on a hurdle, hanged and burnt hanging on the scene of his failure.

Since 1414 the authorities had remained alert and inquisitive. Their victory had been complete and cannot have failed to give them the measure of their opponents. Now and again a Lollard was caught, put on trial and if it was a first offence given the choice between submission and death. These cases have few, if any, original features; just a tragic and monotonous repetition. In 1428 Wycliffe's grave was desecrated, his bones burnt and thrown into the River Swift. Once more, in the spring of 1431, a weaver of Abingdon distributed handbills in London, Salisbury and Coventry advocating the use of the temporalities of the church to relieve tax-payers and meet the wages of the army in France. But the time when such sentiments could receive a sympathetic hearing was past and William Perkins's recklessness cost him his life. That was Lollardy's final attempt to achieve its ends by an appeal to public opinion, by what might be called political action, for many a long day. It had failed to convince the ruling classes that disendowment, especially when advocated by heretical weavers and shoemakers, was politically sound. In future it could only hope to stay alive by remaining inconspicuous.

The fiasco of January 1414 had revealed the treasonable irresponsibility and the numerical insignificance of the heretics. But it had also deprived them of their few surviving leaders of rank and education. It is that that makes it the real turning-point in the history of the sect. Oldcastle's failure meant the final disappearance of the Lollard knight, the landowner of influence and position who had up to then conferred a slight air of respectability upon a movement that was steadily losing caste. Although the losses of the rebels in killed and executed were large considering how few were involved, what made them really crippling was that they included all who were of any social consequence. Lollardy was decapitated; it lost for ever those who could afford its ministers some protection. It never attracted another Oldcastle, hardly, indeed, a landowner of any sort. After 1414 it had no connection with the gentry even on the modest scale that had existed before, so utterly was it discredited.

The massacre of its leaders by Henry V and the hunting down of the remnant by the bishops between 1414 and 1431 destroyed also the last vestiges of its academic tradition. Some graduates like Master John Mybbe put themselves right with their superiors by a hurried conformity that was at least outwardly unshakable; in this they but followed the example of such penitent dons as Repton and Hereford. Others, of whom William Taylor was the most outstanding, were degraded from their orders and degrees and burnt. At Oxford itself continuity had at last been broken and heresy was extinct. When, therefore, Lollardy, kept alive during the worst days of persecution by earnest chaplains and craftsmen in obscure conventicles, once more blossomed in the middle years of the century, it no longer had that sprinkling of university-trained clergy which for forty years after Wycliffe's death had brought some intellectual distinction to the sect. It was, in fact, no longer an Oxford movement; and its founder's subtle theology underwent its final degradation

183

in the unbaked minds of solemn, if well-meaning, bumpkins.

The result of this divorce from the schools can best be illustrated from the views of some of the humbler Lollards preserved in the register of John Chedworth, bishop of Lincoln from 1452 to 1471. Heresy had been revivified in the extreme south of the diocese by the missionary fervour of James Willis, a lettered weaver from Bristol. This successful lay preacher had imbibed his doctrines from William Smith—the third of his name to adorn the sect— a Bristol blacksmith who had lost his life at the stake several years before. The disciple, after a pastorate spent in his native town (where he was compelled to abjure), drifted to London and then finally to Buckinghamshire, to end his days as the apostle of the Chiltern Hills. He not only put new heart into the Lollard congregations at Wycombe, Amersham and Chesham, but won many new converts at Henley, Marlow, Hambledon, Turville and Chinnor. His activities were cut short at last on 13 August 1462, when he was brought to trial before Chedworth at Wooburn. As a lapsed heretic he was bound to suffer death; but though nothing could save him from the flames of this world, he chose once more to abjure in order to die a good Christian.

The crudity of Willis's teaching was well brought out in the trial of one of his flock, William Aylward, of Henley-on-Thames, two years later. The latter had maintained on his own confession that

'the pope of Rome is a great beast and a devil of hell and a synagogue and that he shall lie deeper in hell 9 sithes [i.e. times] than Lucifer; that the Blessed Sacrament of the altar is a great devil of hell and a synagogue, and that he can make as good a sacrament between 2 irons [here speaks the blacksmith] as the priest doth upon his altar; that the blood of Hailes [the relic of Christ's blood preserved at Hailes Abbey, Gloucestershire] is but the blood of a dog [? duck] or a drake; that the king and all those that maintain the church shall go to the devil, and in especial the king because of his great supportation of the church; that there ought no man to be baptised to [i.e. until] he came to old age'.

Such outspoken views, with their contempt for the sacraments, were not exceptional. Others of Willis's followers held that a marriage was made by the consent of the parties without any need for the priest's blessing, that a river or a pond was a better place for baptism than a font and that such things as bell-ringing, singing or the use of organs should be banished from the services of the church. In these voices can be heard the first premonitory snuffle of post-reformation puritanism and the rule of the Saints —and with justice, since an unbroken tradition connects Aylward and his fellow-heretics with the seventeenth-century nonconformists of the Chiltern Hills.

By comparison with the utterances of some Lollards Aylward's iconoclasm seems mild. Thus in 1481 a widow from Ashbourne, Derbyshire, tried before Bishop Hales of Lichfield at Beaudesert, had been heard to deny not only the necessity of baptism for the children of Christians, but also the Virgin Birth. Perhaps the most eccentric belief recorded was that of a butcher of Standon in Hertfordshire, who in 1452 was accused along with a neighbour of maintaining that there was no God save the sun and moon; the fact that he was opposed to baptism and the veneration of images proves that, drunk or sober, he was a Lollard.

It is not surprising that the universities were out of sympathy with such hot-gospellers. This was the price Lollardy had to pay for its loss of an educated priesthood. To fill the void, what had once been the lunatic fringe of the movement inevitably became its centre. A change took place in the reign of Henry VIII, so that by 1530 Bishop Nix of Norwich could say of Gonville Hall in Cambridge that 'no clerk has lately come out of it but savoureth of the frying pan, although he speak never so holily'. But for a century neither of the universities produced a Wycliffite who could have offended the most orthodox palate.

Epilogue

DOCTRINAIRE intellectuals in politics are rarely formidable for long. When Wycliffe died most of the causes for which he had fought so vigorously had been lost, thanks largely to his complete indifference to political strategy. His evolution from schoolman into heretic, at least in its later stages, was as unexpected as it was unwelcome to his aristocratic employers. They were soon doing their best to silence him and to nullify his work. Their success makes it easier to admire his zeal than to forgive him his lack of worldly wisdom.

His catastrophic incompetence as a practical reformer does not, however, in the least embarrass his modern admirers. Doctrinaires, for all the adversity and disillusionment that they suffer in their lives, have one consolation: they may enjoy long after death apotheosis at the hands of equally doctrinaire historians. So it has been with Wycliffe. Thanks to a Reformation he did little or nothing to inspire and in effect everything possible to delay, he has been hailed for centuries as its Morning Star, the herald of its dawn. Yet Wycliffe, in fact, did more than any man in Catholic England—though admittedly that was not his intention—to discredit even moderate reform with the political class which alone had the power to carry it out. As if the Henrician Reformation could have happened against the will of Henry VIII and the men of property! It was impossible without their active co-operation. The successes of Luther and Calvin were a tribute to the political anarchy where their work was done; in England, their shrift would have been as short as Wycliffe's.

Nothing is to be gained by over-estimating the extent of the English heresiarch's achievement. His excesses and, still more, those of his disciples made reform disreputable and prepared the way for the easy triumph of reaction.

Lollardy had always appealed most strongly to the lower middle class; after 1414 that class monopolised it completely. That is why it had very little influence on the Reformation when it came. The establishment of a state church under the supreme headship of the king brought no end to the persecution of the Lollards. Their feeble protest was ultimately drowned in the louder chorus of protestant nonconformity. Their heirs were, in short, not the Anglicans, but the Brownists and the Independents.

This may have been far from their founder's original purpose. For Wycliffe had not very much in common with the weavers of Bristol and the butcher of Standon, whose opinions would perhaps have shocked him. But it was he who first taught them to question the church's sacramental system. He therefore set them on the road that could only lead them to death or an humiliating submission. Yet protestants of many shades from Bale, Foxe and Milton to such latterday writers as Trevelyan and Workman have agreed 'to regard with thankfulness and pride' a ministry so disastrous in its consequences.

It is not surprising that with this naïve approach to history they are also grossly unfair to the men on whom fell the duty of persecution. Credit is rarely given to the bishops for their conscientious efforts to induce their victims to submit or for their reluctance to see even the obstinate go to their deaths. Yet, apart from the loud-mouthed and bloodthirsty Despenser—whose actions in this case were less ruthless than his reported speech—there was no bishop who showed a delight in the sport. Both Courtenay and Arundel set their suffragans an example of scrupulous patience and restraint. Arundel's treatment of Purvey was particularly magnanimous. That a man should be burnt for a refusal to accept the church's teaching as authoritative, we may all now agree, is monstrous. But it was possible to think differently in 1401 without being a monster. Compared with most religious—and some political—persecutors, the bishops of fifteenth-century England were humane, hesitant, almost squeamish. That they have been depicted otherwise since the days of Foxe does not say as much for English historians. Indignation and pity for the martyrs can easily prevent us from doing impartial justice alike to persecutors and persecuted. It is more important to understand than to side instinctively with the under-dog.

Calamitous as were the efforts of Wycliffe as a practical reformer, his life and teaching yet deserve at least as much study as they have received. Whatever mistakes he made as a political strategist, he still remains one of the most remarkable figures of his age. His vitality and the fearlessness of his thought—the very qualities which interfered with his success in action—shine beneath the dust and tarnish of nearly six centuries. Time has reduced most of his great contemporaries to vague, scarcely discernible shapes; Wycliffe, in spite of the enormous gaps in the evidence, lives, if as a force more than as a man. His career has besides a special value for the student of late medieval history. As a scholar, politician, preacher and rebel he touched his times at so many points that to follow him through his various avocations is to learn much that is worth knowing about the England of his day. The Lollard sect may have been hopelessly outmatched, but the fortunes of its hunted and sometimes martyred apostles help us to a better understanding of the society which they strove in vain to alter. For the historian, indeed, the reformation that did not come off is scarcely less interesting than the one that did.

Note on Sources

FOR a century the records have been so industriously searched for evidence upon the life of Wycliffe that only a chance find is now likely to advance our knowledge of this obscure subject. I have made none, and so have had to content myself with sifting and interpreting what others had already brought to light. The fullest and most recent bibliography is that by the late B. L. Manning (*Cambridge Medieval History*, vol. vii, pp. 900–7).

With the Lollards the case is different and much unprinted evidence can still be found. For the first trial of Swinderby I have made extensive use of the Register of Bishop John Buckingham in the Diocesan Record Office at Lincoln (esp. folios. 242–3ᵛ). This also contains useful matter about later outbreaks of heresy at Chipping Warden (fos. 357–7ᵛ) and Northampton (fos. 398 and 406). The chief source for the activities of John Fox is the information laid by Richard Stormsworth (Public Record Office, Ancient Petitions, S.C.8/142/7099), and this I have used in preference to the imperfect translations already printed. On Oldcastle's plot a mass of extremely valuable material survives in the records of the King's Bench. My account is based upon the Ancient Indictments (P.R.O., K.B.9/203–12) and *Coram Rege* Rolls (P.R.O., K.B.27/611–17). Some useful extracts from these and other sources will be found in British Museum MS. Cotton Cleopatra E.II. I have also derived a few minor details from Archbishop Arundel's Register (Lambeth Library, esp. fos. 125, 278 and 293ᵛ), from the Issue Roll for Michaelmas and Hilary terms Henry V (P.R.O., E.403/614), from the corresponding Warrants for Issue (P.R.O., E.404/29), from the Chancery Warrant for the arrest of Swinderby and Bell, 9 March 1392 (P.R.O., C.81/532/7981) and from the Chancery series known as Significations of Excommunication. [P.R.O., C.85, esp. files 11–13 (Canterbury), 91 (Hereford) and 109–11 (Lincoln).]

Suggestions for Further Reading

Craigie, Sir William A., 'The English versions (to Wyclif)' in *The Bible in its Ancient and English Versions*, ed. H. Wheeler Robinson (1940), pp. 128–45.

Deanesly, Margaret, *The Significance of the Lollard Bible* (1951).

Gwynn, Aubrey, *The English Austin Friars in the Time of Wyclif* (1940).

Hamilton Thompson, A., *The English Clergy and their Organisation in the Later Middle Ages* (1947).

Manning, B. L., *The People's Faith in the time of Wyclif* (1919).

Mollat, G., *Les Papes d'Avignon (1305–1378)*, revised edition (1949).

Perroy, Édouard, *L'Angleterre et le Grand Schisme d'Occident* (1933).

Poole, Reginald Lane, *Illustrations of the History of Medieval Thought and Learning*, revised edition (1920).

Richardson, H. G., 'Heresy and the Lay Power under Richard II' in *English Historical Review*, vol. LI. (1936), pp. 1–28.

Salter, H. E., *Medieval Oxford* (1936).

Steel, Anthony, *Richard II* (1941).

Tout, T. F., *Chapters in the Administrative History of Medieval England*, vols. III and IV (1928), chapters IX and X.

Waugh, W. T., 'Sir John Oldcastle', in *English Historical Review*, vol. XX (1905), pp. 434–56 and 637–58.

Waugh, W. T., 'The Great Statute of Praemunire', ibid., vol. XXXVII (1922), pp. 173–205.

Wood-Legh, K. L., *Studies in Church Life in England under Edward III* (1934).

Index

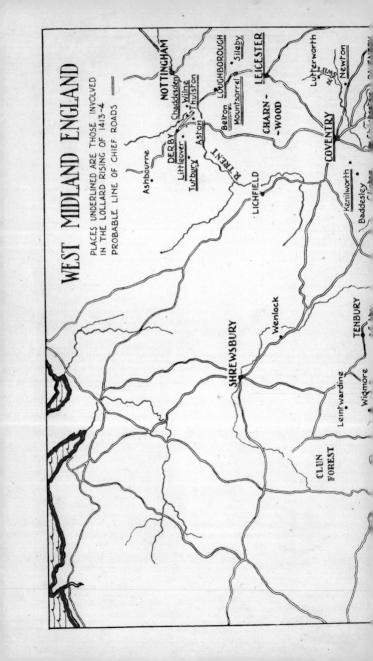

WEST MIDLAND ENGLAND

PLACES UNDERLINED ARE THOSE INVOLVED
IN THE LOLLARD RISING OF 1413-4
PROBABLE LINE OF CHIEF ROADS ————

NOTTINGHAM

LOUGHBOROUGH   Sileby

DERBY

Cheddesden   Wilne

Thulston

LEICESTER

Belton   Mountsorrel

Littleover   Aston

Turbury

CHARN-
~WOOD

Lutterworth

Newton

Ashbourne

R. TRENT

COVENTRY

LICHFIELD

Kenilworth

Baddesley

Wenlock

SHREWSBURY

TENBURY

Leintwardine

Wigmore

CLUN
FOREST